PRAISE FOR THE WORLD BECOMES WHAT WE TEACH

"This book has inspired us to re-examine our educational philosophy, approach, and practices. We have transformed our programs for teachers, administrators, and youth so that they are solutionary. We've also launched an annual Solutionary Fair based on the ideas in this book. The impact that solutionary teaching and learning have had on driving environmental and social change in our schools and communities is immeasurable."
—**Andra Yeghoian**, Environmental Literacy and Sustainability Coordinator & Doron Markus, Ed.D., Career and STEM Success Coordinator, San Mateo County Office of Education

"This book has never been more important. It provides us with a healing vision for a world struggling under the weight of racism, environmental exploitation, and a host of other ills, and it outlines a powerful and practical pathway forward for all teachers and schools committed to preparing children to be the next caretakers of our planet. Zoe Weil's solutionary approach takes Problem-Based Learning to the next level by including not just critical and creative thinking but systems thinking and ethical analysis. It calls on us to go beyond simply preparing students to be 'college and career ready' and to prepare them as well to contribute to the creation of a just, healthy, and sustainable world where all living beings can thrive. Never before have we needed such a strong moral vision for our children or for our schools. I urge my fellow educators to read this book and to join together to make it foundational to our teaching."—**Steve Cochrane**, former Superintendent of the Year, Princeton Public Schools

"*The World Becomes What We Teach* is powerful. I call it Problem-Based Learning on natural steroids! Educators who plant seeds of humaneness inspired by the lessons in Zoe's book can create the conditions for a world of possibilities. We will then reap a world full of hope and purposeful intentionality that is care-full!" —**José Torres**, Author and President, Illinois Mathematics and Science Academy

"Zoe Weil's clear and compelling vision offers an urgent challenge to all of us about the purpose of education—one that we ignore at great peril."—**Julie Meltzer**, 2019 Maine Curriculum Leader of the Year

"In an increasingly polarized world, this book is a ray of hope inspiring a generation of solutionaries in our schools to tackle our most pressing problems."—**Akash Patel**, Global Teacher Prize Finalist, UNA-USA National Council Member

"*The World Becomes What We Teach* offers a practical roadmap for implementing education that empowers children with the necessary knowledge, skills, and zeal to thrive in today's world. Zoe Weil provides the reader with a robust framework for building a future that is more humane, just, peaceful, and sustainable."—**Victoria Chiatula**, Ph.D., CEO & Founder EdPro International

"*The World Becomes What We Teach* may be the most important book, with both the simplest and most powerful answers, to address the challenges we face in our world effectively, meaningfully, and positively. If we heed Zoe Weil's call to educate a generation of solutionaries, we will witness the unfolding of a truly just, compassionate, and healthy world. Read this book for the sake of any children you love and the future of us all."—**Matt Goldman**, Co-founder Blue Man Group and Blue School

"An amazingly articulated big picture, as well as a practical guide, for educational leaders, teachers, and parents around the world. An inspiring and timely vision of what's possible for K–12 education and our collective future."—**Mike Johnston**, Ph.D., Assistant Head of School, Frankfurt International School, Steering Committee, Compass Education for a Sustainable Future

"A common-sense vision for how schooling should be. If we want a better world for our progeny, we would do well to take Weil's inspiring, thoughtful ideas as far and as fast as possible."—**Seth Berry**, former Majority Leader, Maine State Legislature and former teacher

"In light of the need for lifelong learning in a changing world, Zoe Weil's call to 'adopt a more relevant and meaningful purpose for schooling; make schools real world- and solutionary-focused; and prepare teachers to educate their students to be solutionaries,' is logical and essential. The evidence is clear that this kind of teaching and learning is already happening. There are a great many stories of children and young people contributing to a healthy, humane, and sustainable future through school, and many examples of what educators can do to make this happen. Zoe illustrates why schools need to change and then shows us what the new narrative looks like. It is compelling. This book will change you."—**Jaimie P. Cloud**, President, The Cloud Institute for Sustainability Education

"This book takes on conventional reformist thinking, unfetters the educational imagination, and repositions the very notion of 'relevance' in schooling to meet the critical issues of this era on Earth. Zoe opens a doorway onto a new landscape for teaching, learning, the development of curriculum, and the purpose of schooling itself. Then she hands us a map, a GPS, and travel guide. This book, once well dog-eared and coffee-stained, should grace the shelves of any educator or transformational leader truly committed to children, the Earth, and a just, sustainable society."—**Khalif Williams**, Director, The Bay School

"Zoe Weil is an important player in the emerging worldwide movement to make education more about applying our newly empowered young people's passions and capabilities to making their world a better place. I hope that this book informs the thinking and practice of as many parents and educators as possible, that a great many Solutionary Schools get created and thrive in the world, and that my son grows up in a world full of solutionaries—and becomes one!"—**Marc Prensky**, Founder and Executive Director, The Global Future Education Foundation and Institute

"Imagine if Zoe Weil's vision was the default setting for a system of schools and communities creating learning environments rich with joy, curiosity, complexity, and an undeniable belief that we are all capable—from student to community—in making a positive, long-term impact on the world around us. Better, imagine if you—the reader—realizes that this book is your invitation to be both a solutionary in your own life and a co-conspirator in creating a system of solutionary schools in communities far and wide. This is Zoe Weil's belief. And this is your invitation to co-design a remarkable future for students, teachers, schools, and communities ahead."—**Christian Long**, Founding Partner, WONDER, By Design: A learning and design expedition

"Zoe Weil asks the questions we need to thoughtfully answer not only for our system of education but also for our future on this planet. I have worked in education for over 25 years, from experiential outdoor education to service-learning in classroom settings. Weil's model and vision is more oriented toward effective systems thinking than any other approach to education I have encountered. This book serves as a guide to action and will help us make school meaningful, joyful, and solutionary."—**Barbara Fiore**, Education Consultant, Former Program Director, Hurricane Island Outward Bound School

"Zoe Weil sees a world the rest of us are still struggling to make out—one that is more equitable, restorative, and compassionate, and one in which we are all more empathetic and at peace. *The World Becomes What We Teach* is a manifesto for the future of education, and a series of recipes for teaching children that a humane world is not just possible—it's inevitable, as long as we help young people engage in work that provides a slice of the solution, and a way of discovering their most authentic selves."—**Sam Chaltain**, Author of *Faces of Learning* and Coproducer of *A Year at Mission Hill*

"Zoe Weil offers a vision for education that is based on respect for children's curiosity, creativity, and capabilities. She shows how educational practices can be based on genuine hope and shares a blueprint for how to reform education with imagination, rigor, and love for the world. This is a brilliant, necessary, uplifting book."—**Kathleen Roberts Skerrett**, Dean of Arts and Sciences, University of Richmond

"*The World Becomes What We Teach* is the work of a visionary educator that questions a traditional, competitive approach to education and offers one based on cooperation and collaboration. Not only is it a powerful indictment of how our schools inhibit creativity and critical thinking, her pedagogy empowers students to imagine and create the world they want. I highly recommend this book to educators, parents, and anyone who wants to make the world a better place." —**Arnold Greenberg**, Founder, Miquon Upper School, Deep Run School of Homesteading and Community, and Liberty School—A Democratic Learning Community

"If you want to learn how we can create an education system and a world that is more humane, peaceful, equitable, and resilient, you must read this book. It might just cause you to reevaluate your assumptions about living and learning." —**Nikhil Goyal**, author of *Schools on Trial: How Freedom and Creativity Can Fix Our Educational Malpractice*

"This is an important book from an important thinker in the

field of education. Zoe's original ideas are based on decades of practical hands-on work. She creates an optimistic vision of what can be if we are willing to rethink educational models to meet the needs of our twenty-first-century world."—**Doug Alexander**, President, Actua Corporation

"Zoe Weil goes beyond the rhetoric in debates about improving education and challenges us to revamp the very purpose of schools. As an educator, lawyer, entrepreneur, and mentor, I was excited by her approach. As a long-time advocate and a parent of Model UN students, I love her vision of new and more challenging Solutionary clubs for today's students. *Why* should students research and debate imaginary issues when the world is ripe with real problems? Zoe Weil logically describes how this generation can be challenged and trained to create solutions to problems for the betterment of the world and the future of all living creatures. I loved this book and plan to share it with parents, educators, researchers, and students."—**Nancy Hodari**, Founder and Education Director, Equilibrium Studio

"I believe we all have a unique capacity for contribution. However, too frequently schools stifle children's resolve to express it. Zoe Weil's approach to schooling, as laid out in her book *The World Becomes What We Teach*, skillfully identifies how to nurture this seed of goodness while simultaneously providing students with all of the tools required to flourish in the twenty-first century. Her collaborative, interdisciplinary approach to education could very well be the prescription needed to cultivate a generation of 'Solutionaries' ready to take on the greatest societal challenges of our time."—**Ariel Nessel**, Founder, The Pollination Project

THE WORLD BECOMES WHAT WE TEACH

*Educating a Generation
of Solutionaries*

ZOE WEIL

Lantern Publishing & Media ● Brooklyn, New York

2021
Lantern Publishing & Media
128 Second Place
Brooklyn, NY 11231
www.lanternpm.org

This title was previously published by Booklight Inc. (DBA Lantern Books). In December 2019, Booklight Inc. transferred all its assets, including this book, to Lantern Publishing & Media, a new company dedicated to the same publishing mission as Lantern Books.

Printed in the United States of America

Names: Weil, Zoe, author.
Title: The world becomes what we teach : educating a generation of solutionaries / Zoe Weil.
Description: New York : Lantern Books, 2016. | Includes bibliographical references.
Identifiers: LCCN 2016004450 (print) | LCCN 2016009329 (ebook) | ISBN 9781590565186 (pbk. : alk. paper) | ISBN 9781590565193 (epub)
Subjects: LCSH: Educational psychology. | Change (Psychology) | Environmental education.
Classification: LCC LB1051 .W2865 2016 (print) | LCC LB1051 (ebook) | DDC 371.102—dc23
LC record available at http://lccn.loc.gov/2016004450

Education is not the filling of a pail, but the lighting of a fire.—**William Butler Yeats**

Students will achieve at levels far beyond what is expected if you give them the opportunity.—**Esther Wojcicki**

The purpose of education should be the development of a world that works for all living beings.—**Dr. Shariff Abdullah**

Every good teacher has hundreds of heirs. Perhaps this is the best reason to teach.—**Dexter Chapin**

CONTENTS

Solutionary [suh-LOO-shuh ner-ee]

Noun

1. A person who identifies inhumane, unjust, unsustainable systems and then develops solutions to transform them so that they are restorative, healthy, and equitable for people, animals, and the environment.

2. A person who brings critical, systems, strategic, and creative thinking to bear on pressing and entrenched challenges in an effort to create positive changes that do not harm one group while helping another.

3. A person who strives to make personal choices and support systems that do the most good and least harm for all people, animals, and the environment.

Adjective

1. Pertaining to or characterized by solving problems in a strategic, comprehensive way that does not harm one group while helping another.

2. Innovative and far-reaching in a positive way for people, animals, and the environment.

PREFACE

Dear 4th Grade Class of P.S. 165,

As you are starting your solutionary efforts, we want you to know that your work is all about having fun while helping change the world. We, the middle school TEAK Class 18, have just begun our own solutionary projects ourselves, and it has been amazing. We have learned many things, and this is what we want you to know as you too try to find solutions for the world.

Your solutions must be friendly to all beings on Earth. No matter how you try to solve a problem, you must make sure your solution does not hurt people, the environment, animals, or anything else. A solutionary solution must get to the source of the problem and fix it from there and not just reduce the problem. Though this sounds like hard work, it definitely can be done!

We encourage you all to take positive risks and remember your goals and passions as you begin to change the world for the better. One day you'll look back on the changes you've made in the world and smile. You'll be astonished to learn that children, no matter what age, can change the world! We wish you luck on your journey to be problem solvers and hope you succeed. If you fail in some ways, you must use your failures as a springboard and continue working. We hope to work with you all and get to know you so we can create a better world together! As Norman Vincent

Peale said, "Shoot for the moon. Even if you miss, you'll land amongst the stars."

With Heart,

Angela Osei-Ampadu
Grade 7, and TEAK Class 18
New York City

INTRODUCTION

I believe that it's possible to create a just, healthy, and peaceful world; to develop sustainable and humane energy, food, economic, transportation, production, construction, and other systems; to end poverty; and to ensure that everyone is treated equitably. I believe that we can learn to resolve conflicts without violence; to treat other people and nonhuman animals with respect and compassion; to slow the rate of extinction; and to restore ecosystems. And I believe—based on thirty-five years of experience—that there is a clear, practical, and positive path to achieve this vision. This book shares that path.

The solutions to the problems we face will come when we effectively and wisely transform the system of education. As Mahatma Gandhi said, "If we are to reach real peace in the world . . . we shall have to begin with the children." The education of children is the root system underlying other societal systems, and for the sake of our children and the world, I believe that we must:

1. Adopt a more relevant and meaningful purpose for schooling.
2. Make schools real world– and solutionary-focused.
3. Prepare teachers to educate their students to be solutionaries.

3

If we can successfully achieve these three goals, there is every reason to believe that we can create a world where all can thrive. This belief in the power of education to prepare students to be solutionaries—people who bring knowledge and skills to bear on pressing and entrenched challenges in an effort to create positive change—stems from my work as a humane educator. Humane education examines the interconnected issues of human rights, environmental sustainability, and animal protection, with the goal of fostering compassion, inspiring kindness and responsibility, and preparing students to solve problems in ways that are good for all people, animals, and the ecosystems that sustain life. Humane educators help students gain the knowledge, tools, and motivation to be conscientious choice-makers and engaged change-makers for a better future.

In 1989, I created a humane education program that offered presentations, classes, and afterschool courses, primarily in and around Philadelphia, PA. By the mid-1990s, we were reaching approximately 10,000 middle and high school students annually. Almost everywhere we taught, there were young people eager to take action, start school clubs, and make positive contributions.

Although it was rewarding to see our programs have an impact, they were add-ons, rather than the core of school curricula. I realized that unless the educational approach in the U.S. and beyond shifted significantly, we would be hard-pressed to solve the challenges that confront us. So, in 1996 I co-founded the Institute for Humane Education (IHE), primarily to train and provide professional development to educators wanting to teach about interconnected global ethical issues, infuse their curricula and classes with more relevance and meaning, foster compassion and kindness, and prepare their students to solve real-world problems. IHE created the first graduate programs in comprehensive humane education (M.Ed., M.A., Ed.D., Graduate Certificate) in the United States—now offered online through an affiliation with Antioch University—as well as a Solutionary Micro-credential Program, workshops, and free solutionary guidebooks, curricula, and lesson plans for educators everywhere.

Our objectives at IHE include:

- Promoting changes in education that will lead to a world where all people, animals, and nature can survive and thrive;
- Providing the tools, resources, and preparation for educators and schools to fully embrace and implement such changes;
- Preparing young people to become effective solutionaries able to bring about a healthy and just future.

The purpose of this book is to make the case for these objectives and provide ideas about how to achieve them.

What could the outcomes of solutionary learning look like?

Twelve-year-old Kiara is very excited to get to school. She and her classmates have been exploring the answer to this question: *How is it possible that a fast-food burger and an organic apple sometimes cost the same amount of money?* Kiara has found it fascinating to learn about the various agricultural, political, corporate, and economic systems involved in the answer to this question and has been researching the many factors that impact costs of food, gaining skills in critical and systems thinking, reading comprehension, math, civic engagement, and research methods. In the process, she has also become more media literate and aware of the psychology of advertising.

Kiara and her classmates are developing proposed legislation to address and end government subsidies of unhealthy, unsustainably produced foods, and they have secured upcoming appointments with their congressional representative and senators. Kiara has been preparing her presentation to her legislators and is eager to share her knowledge, perspectives, and ideas with them.

* * *

At twenty-eight years old, Alexis has just received her Ph.D. in chemistry and has been hired by a company developing innovative materials for use in the electronics industry. Her research focuses on the elimination of toxins in electronic components and the development of recyclable and biodegradable materials when the individual units are no longer functional.

Alexis traces her interest in chemistry to eighth grade when her class examined a week's worth of school trash. Her teacher had asked how each item in the trash could be avoided by making different purchasing choices; or reused, composted, or recycled. Alexis realized that if she drank tap water instead of juice or didn't buy anything that was wrapped in plastic or Styrofoam, she would produce less waste, but the truth was that she really liked drinking juice and wanted plenty of things that were over-packaged. As her class discussed how they could reduce their trash, Alexis mused that it would be nice if containers and packaging could be composted like food waste and turned into soil. Her teacher said this was a great idea and told her that there were companies working to achieve this goal.

Alexis contacted an inventor developing environmentally responsible packaging, expressing her interest in learning more. Through her dialogue with the inventor, her conversations with her teacher, and her own research, Alexis developed her strong interest in chemistry, which she pursued through subjects she studied both in school and through an internship with the inventor. The seeds planted in middle school and nourished throughout high school and college led to a meaningful and highly valuable career.

* * *

Seven-year-old Elijah is lying on his belly with his chin propped up by his hands on a bed of soft pine needles in a park near his school. He's so quiet and still that he's able to hear and observe woodland animals all around him. A squirrel is chewing on a mushroom only a few yards away. He watches, mesmerized, until the sound of a woodpecker distracts him. He rolls on his back to watch the bird pound her beak into a tree. A few minutes later his face breaks into a huge smile when he notices a small screech owl sleeping in a previously hollowed woodpecker hole.

When he began spending time in the woods, Elijah didn't notice these things. In fact, he squirmed and complained to his teacher when she first brought his class to the park. Over time, however, he's become very observant, and visiting the park is one of his favorite things to do. When he and his classmates return to school, they share their observations and their questions.

On this particular day, Elijah is wondering:

- How can the squirrel eat a mushroom that might be poisonous to people?
- How come the woodpecker's brain doesn't get scrambled by hitting the wood so hard?
- Why is the screech owl sleeping in the middle of the day?

The children have a growing question list on the wall, which they learn to answer through books, Internet searches, and during conversations with their teacher and the naturalist who works at the park. Sometimes students with the same questions work together to find the answers. Usually, the answers lead to more questions, and every outing strengthens their knowledge, heightens their curiosity, and deepens their reverence and appreciation for the natural world. Elijah and his classmates are also learning how to make choices that help protect the park and the animals who reside there.

* * *

Eighteen-year-old Ramon is a high school senior, passionate about issues of justice. He's been dedicated to learning about human rights issues in school. Over the years he has done research and conducted projects on modern-day slavery, child labor, migrant farm work, and the disenfranchisement and oppression of girls and women. Every time he learns about these issues, he becomes involved in educating others. A poet, he has performed his social justice poetry for audiences in and out of school, and several of his YouTube videos have been viewed tens of thousands of times.

At the end of his junior year, Ramon became especially interested in the criminal justice and prison systems in the United States. He learned that the criminal justice system isn't actually just, and that the U.S. incarceration rate is the highest in the world, with U.S. jails housing more than twenty percent of the world's prisoners,[1] who are disproportionately low-income people of color. He now spends time each week interning with a mentor in restorative justice, which helps offenders repair the harm they have caused rather than simply serve time in prison. With a group of classmates, he proposed a new disciplinary policy for his school based on these restorative justice practices, which the school adopted.

Ramon plans to go to college and then law school. When asked about a future career, he says he would like to be a judge. He wants to have a positive impact on the criminal justice system, to address persistent racism and classism within it, and to shift the system away from incarceration and punishment toward restitution and accountability to both the individuals harmed as well as the community at large, and toward the healthy re-entry of formerly incarcerated

---

1   From the *World Prison Population List*, 10th Edition, published by the International Centre for Prison Studies, partner of the University of Essex.

people into educational programs and productive work that pays a living wage. Understanding that certain social and economic systems give rise to violence and criminal acts, his intention is to work to support policies that reduce criminality while helping to make the criminal justice system truly fair, effective, and humane so that it protects society and individuals alike. When asked why he is so dedicated to these goals, he responds, "I just want everyone to succeed."

* * *

I've taken liberties with these stories, although they are based on students I have known and schools that have provided the kind of education that leads to such outcomes. You probably know young people like Kiara, Alexis, Elijah, and Ramon, who have been educated by teachers dedicated to ensuring their students gain such experiences, knowledge, and skills. To solve the challenges we face, we need caring, curious, motivated young people who have had the opportunity to solve real-world problems. Where will they come from? They will come from schools that are prepared and committed to educating a generation of solutionaries.[2]

Transforming our educational system won't be easy, but I believe that it is the most important and strategic path toward creating more just, peaceful, and sustainable societies. Because the world inevitably becomes what we teach, it's up to each of us—whether we are teachers, school

---

2   I introduced this concept during my first TEDx talk, "The World Becomes What You Teach," https://www.youtube.com/watch?v=t5HEV96dIuY.

administrators, parents, grandparents, concerned citizens, legislators, entrepreneurs and business leaders, or any number of other professionals—to commit to transforming schooling so that it is truly worthy of children and genuinely worthwhile for the world they will both inherit and shape.

PART I

WHY AND HOW SCHOOLS MUST CHANGE

What are the root challenges in education?

Most people in industrialized countries have experienced thirteen years of formal schooling, so it is not surprising that many consider themselves to be legitimate critics of education.

Our feelings about schooling run the gamut. Some believe that if the curriculum and pedagogy were good enough for them, they should be good enough for children today. Others remember school as primarily anxiety-provoking and often boring. They know that the opportunities to learn today are abundant and exciting, making traditional approaches to education outdated.

While our perspectives are shaped in part by our memories of school, as well as our children's experiences, they are also shaped by our zip codes. Because public schools in the U.S. are funded in large part through property tax revenues, people in higher-income areas have better-funded schools than people in lower-income areas.[1]

In communities across the U.S., schools have become more rather than less segregated over the past half-century.[2] The promise of equal educational opportunities for all has shown itself to be illusory. Racist practices and attitudes that have led to segregated neighborhoods, as well as income disparities, perpetuate educational inequities. Moreover, while the majority of students in public schools are non-white, according to a 2016 government report only eighteen percent of teachers are people of color.[3]

There are several reasons[4] for this and many efforts to change it, because studies show that having teachers who represent a similar background, race, and ethnicity to the majority of their students makes a positive difference for

---

1   See Alana Samuels, "Good School, Rich School; Bad School, Poor School," *The Atlantic*, August 25, 2016, https://www.theatlantic.com/business/archive/2016/08/property-taxes-and-unequal-schools/497333.

2   To teach about school segregation see, Keith Meatto, "Still Separate, Still Unequal: Teaching about School Segregation and Educational Inequality," *New York Times*, May 2, 2019, https://www.nytimes.com/2019/05/02/learning/lesson-plans/still-separate-still-unequal-teaching-about-school-segregation-and-educational-inequality.html.

3   See U.S. Department of Education report, *The State of Racial Diversity in the Educator Workforce*: https://www2.ed.gov/rschstat/eval/highered/racial-diversity/state-racial-diversity-workforce.pdf.

4   See Josh Moss, "Where Are All the Teachers of Color?" *Harvard Ed. Magazine* Summer 2016 https://www.gse.harvard.edu/news/ed/16/05/where-are-all-teachers-color.

both children and their communities.[5] To be clear, fully representative schools aren't just good for children of color; they are good for all children, education, and society as a whole.

Discriminatory discipline of young people and "zero-tolerance" policies have resulted in a pattern of suspensions and expulsions, sometimes for minor infractions, primarily among Black and Hispanic students. These policies have led to a pernicious school-to-prison pipeline.[6] While restorative justice practices (like those Ramon proposed for his school in the Introduction) are being adopted in more and more schools, and the harsh disciplinary trend is starting to reverse, schools often still promote "tough love" approaches. As one teacher posted on Twitter: "I was told that 'these kids' need to be handled very firmly with high expectation and rigidity. That didn't sit well with me, but I tried it and failed. My style now is 'love with reckless abandon,' and I see high achievement/growth."[7]

The COVID-19 pandemic dramatically revealed a number of other gaps and divides. With the closing of schools, many children dependent upon in-person schooling for two meals a day were left hungry as schools scrambled to figure out how to provide them with food. Those young people

---

5   See Andre Perry, "Black Teachers Matter, for Students and Communities," *The Hechinger Report*, September 17, 2019, https://hechingerreport.org/black-teachers-matter-for-students-and-communities.

6   See Libby Nelson and Dara Lind, "The School to Prison Pipeline Explained," Justice Policy Initiative, February 24, 2015, http://www.justicepolicy.org/news/8775.

7   Trina Parrish @BlasterOfArt on Twitter, December 9, 2020.

without Internet and computer access at home were unable to participate in remote learning and hybrid models of education, and schools and teachers were often unequipped to support them. While high-income families were able to form pods and hire private teachers to educate their children, low-income families were not. *Millions* of children disappeared from school entirely during the pandemic.[8] The pandemic exposed profound inequities and put on display the burden placed on schools and teachers to solve deeply entrenched systems of racism, economic inequality, and educational inequities.

The issues above need our dedicated attention. At the same time, this book is based on the premise that education needs not only to be made fully equitable, but also to be *re-imagined*. Fundamentally, we are not yet preparing students for life and work in a technologically changing, globalized world, nor for a future in which much of life on Earth faces dire threats. Despite our many and various critiques of education, we often miss some of the most crucial underlying issues as well as some of the most exciting opportunities for transformation. For example:

- It's not just that many students are graduating from high school without the necessary skills in literacy, numeracy, and science; it's that even if they were to graduate with *exceptional* skills, they would not by design or purpose be properly educated and

---

8   See Stacey Ritzen, "How Many Kids Have Not Gone Back to School Since the Pandemic Began?" n.d. *Nautilus*: https://coronavirus.nautil.us/missing-school-coronavirus-pandemic.

prepared for today's world and the important task of solving critical global problems.

- It's not just that many students drop out; it's that often these students perceive school to be irrelevant and not worthwhile, and many students—even those who don't drop out—are largely disengaged.

- It's not just that there is an "achievement gap"; it's that there is an *opportunity* gap, and we continue to fail to address poverty and racism, which are the primary causes of that gap, and often use biased standards and assessment tools to measure achievement. Simultaneously, we fail to identify and measure many other achievements that matter.

- It's not just that students aren't performing up to par; it's that standardized tests are often poor evaluation tools, unworthy of our students' true needs, and often at odds with helping them gain many of the skills they require. Many public-school teachers are required to "teach to the test" and are rarely provided with preparation to educate about interconnected global issues and teach solutionary thinking skills that are so essential for their students, their country, and the world.

- It's not just that bullying is a problem in schools and that compassion and character are not adequately cultivated to ensure kindness and responsibility; it's that our daily lives are inextricably connected through the global economy to institutionalized brutality, injustice, and environmental devastation, and that we do not usually learn in school how to be kind and responsible in a far-reaching way in a world in which our everyday choices impact other people, animals, and ecosystems across the planet.[9]

- It's not just that cheating is rampant in school; it's that we have an outmoded system that tempts students to cheat. With facts literally at their fingertips, students most need to cultivate skills in research, collaboration, and critical, systems, strategic, creative, scientific, logical, and design thinking. These skills are most effectively taught and fostered in ways that are antithetical to cheating, and teachers need support to shift their focus toward these skills and employing more relevant assessments that make cheating a non-issue.

- It's not just that many students are overly stressed by their packed schedules, their hours of homework, and their extracurricular obligations; it's that they have little opportunity to connect their learning to the real world, develop and follow their own passions, and contribute in ways that are truly meaningful and demonstrate real accomplishments.

- It's not just that so many schools aren't succeeding at achieving their stated objectives; it's that many of their stated objectives are no longer the right ones for today's world.

---

9   Educators who want to teach about the impacts of everyday choices on others far removed may be met with resistance from parents who do not want their family choices to be challenged in school.

Thus, when we hear in the media and from politicians about the problems with today's schools, it's essential that we look beyond the sound bites to recognize and understand the limitations of these critiques. We need to shift away from politically motivated side-taking and set our sights on solutions to education that are most meaningful to *all* students and their futures; that are truly helpful to the profession of teaching; and that are ultimately best for the world our children will soon be influencing.

With this said, it's important to stress that many teachers, school administrators, instructional and curriculum designers, and district leaders are trying to create learning environments and curricula that better prepare students for today's and tomorrow's world. Despite often being thwarted by systems outside their control, they are working tirelessly and creatively. We owe these educators a great debt, and they deserve our full support.

Let's shift the purpose of schooling.

In the United States the current purpose of schooling is expressed in the mission statement at the U.S. Department of Education website: *to promote student achievement and preparation for global competitiveness by fostering educational excellence and ensuring equal access.* Is this mission sufficient and appropriate for students whose future is threatened by global problems they will be required to address? Might they be better served by a more meaningful and comprehensive mission that includes learning to solve the challenges they will face?

Climate change is not a future possibility; it is happening now,[10] with catastrophic impacts on humans and nonhumans alike.[11] Human population continues to grow, and of the nearly 8 billion people in the world, more than 700 million live in extreme poverty on less than $1.90 per day,[12] and approximately 40 million are enslaved.[13] While disenfranchised groups have gained critical legal rights and protections, racism, sexism, homophobia/transphobia and other forms of oppression and prejudice persist not only in the hearts and minds of individuals but within institutional structures. Animals, too, are facing horrific exploitation and cruelty. Tens of billions of land animals[14] and trillions of sea animals[15] suffer and die each year as part of an unsustainable and inhumane global food system. Meanwhile, misinformation, disinformation, and polarization impact

---

10 See Intergovernmental Panel on Climate Change, *AR6 Synthesis Report: Climate Change 2022*, http://www.ipcc.ch/publications_and_data/publications_and_data_reports.shtml.

11 See National Museum of Natural History, "Extinction Over Time," n.d., https://naturalhistory.si.edu/education/teaching-resources/paleontology/extinction-over-time.

12 See World Vision, "What Is Poverty?" n.d., https://www.worldvision.org/sponsorship-news-stories/global-poverty-facts#what-is-poverty.

13 See Free the Slaves, "Slavery in History," n.d., https://www.freetheslaves.net/about-slavery/slavery-in-history.

14 See Alex Thornton, "This Is How Many Animals We Eat Each Year," World Economic Forum, February 8, 2019, https://www.weforum.org/agenda/2019/02/chart-of-the-day-this-is-how-many-animals-we-eat-each-year.

15 See FishCount.org.uk, "Fish Count Estimates," n.d., http://fishcount.org.uk/fish-count-estimates#wildestimate.

our ability to accurately identify and collaboratively address these and other challenges.

Despite the grim realities above, we've seen real progress and have ever-expanding opportunities to solve our problems. For example, people in countries around the globe are living longer and more materially secure lives,[16] and (media reports notwithstanding) there is less violence toward people than ever before in recorded human history.[17] Only in this century have we had the capacity to communicate and collaborate instantaneously with so many across the globe. Even in many countries where poverty is pervasive, mobile phone access is enabling millions to connect with others worldwide and to access the growing body of knowledge humans are creating and disseminating. There are also exciting innovations occurring in green technology, architecture, construction, and production. Clean energy systems and regenerative farming practices are expanding, and people in every country are devising solutions to what have been seemingly intractable problems. And thanks in large part to positive changes within the education system, young people are growing consistently less racist, sexist, homophobic/ transphobic and more philanthropic and environmentally conscious.[18]

---

16 See Professor of International Health Hans Rosling's short video for the BBC graphing health and wealth trends over time: https://www.youtube.com/watch?v=jbkSRLYSojo.

17 See Harvard professor Steven Pinker's book, *The Better Angels of Our Nature: Why Violence Has Declined*. New York: Viking Press, 2011.

18 See Tom Jacobs, "Americans Are Becoming Less Racist and Homophobic, According to New Research," *Pacific Standard*,

In other words, today's world presents our children with unprecedented challenges as well as unprecedented opportunities. Our ability to acquire pertinent information, share our knowledge, work together to solve our challenges, and create a more just and healthy world is real and growing. Yes, we face potential disasters, systemic injustices, and widespread cruelties, and yes, through the right kind of education, we can solve these problems. Given all these factors, doesn't it make sense for schools to ensure that students understand the formidable challenges before them; prepare young people to address these challenges; and engage youth in cultivating their ability and desire to create meaningful solutions to potentially calamitous global problems?

Henry David Thoreau once said, "There are a thousand hacking at the branches of evil to one who is striking at the root." Because the education of children is the root system underlying other societal systems, it is critical that we reexamine and shift the purpose of schooling. If schools were actually successful at achieving the current U.S. Department of Education's mission—so that graduates were all able to compete effectively in the global economy—these young people would likely perpetuate and perhaps even escalate the global problems we face. However, if we embrace a mission more worthy of our children and their future—to prepare them to be engaged and knowledgeable solutionaries for an equitable, humane, and sustainable world—we will have a purpose that propels us toward a deeply meaningful and

---

January 7, 2019, https://psmag.com/social-justice/americans-are-becoming-less-racist-and-homophobic.

relevant education that benefits both youth and all on Earth. Our children are far more likely to be successful and happy if they have the knowledge, skills, and motivation to effectively address and solve the problems they will face through whatever careers and jobs they choose to pursue. Just as what harms our world harms our children, what benefits our world benefits our children. This is why we must commit to educating a generation of solutionaries.

What should we teach?

Given the reality of globalization, constantly evolving technologies, rapidly shifting job opportunities, and a planet in peril, it's important to re-evaluate the body of knowledge and skill sets that we require children to obtain. It helps to come to this task with a beginner's eyes, unfettered by attachments to traditional subjects, content areas, and skill development. With limited hours in the day, and in a world where information about virtually anything and everything is readily available, what essential knowledge and skills should students acquire and why? The answer to this question should change over time. Skill sets that were once valuable may not be essential in today's world, while other skill sets are now vital. Content knowledge that is important today may be eclipsed by other content knowledge in the coming decades. This is why transferable skills, understandings, and habits of mind are so critical, and why memorizing specific facts has become largely outdated.[19]

---

19 Watch Dan Brown's short video for a young man's perspective on the value of learning facts in the twenty-first century, https://www.youtube.com/watch?v=E3jjI15RXtc.

A thought experiment quickly reinforces the problem of primarily focusing on content at all. Consider which of the following you believe are subjects that all children should study in the U.S., recognizing, of course, that the myriad subtopics under these general subject headings should evoke the same question:

biology; chemistry; physics; ecology and environmental science; geology; botany; nutrition; mycology; astronomy; neuroscience; ethology and zoology; oceanography and marine science; climate science and climate change; engineering; computer science and technologies; ancient history; U.S. history, governance, and civics; history of other continents, regions, and nations; history of colonization; history of indigenous peoples; history of war, peace, and nonviolent movements; history of caste, slavery, racism, anti-Semitism, sexism, homophobia, and other manifestations of prejudice and oppression; heroic leaders and change agents throughout history; inventions that changed history; overview of human history from the beginning of time to the present; art history; geography and its impacts on cultures; world religions; geometry; algebra; calculus and trigonometry; statistics and probability; anthropology; archeology; psychology; sociology; money and economics; social entrepreneurship; American and English literature; drama; mythology; visual arts; poetry; music; world languages; world literature in translation; the classics; philosophy;

logic and epistemology; movements for justice and rights; media, disinformation, and conspiracy theories; physical and mental health; the true cost of our product, food, and clothing choices; sustainable and ethical living in a globalized world.

What did you find yourself thinking and feeling as you read this list? My hope is that you felt confused and uncertain, perhaps overwhelmed, and that this long (and by no means exhaustive) list called into question the basic subject categories that we currently teach in U.S. schools. I also hope you found yourself wondering why we teach what we teach.

I believe that mandatory school subjects ought to vary based on where one lives in the world and available opportunities, and that students should learn a little about many subjects. But far more important than specific content are the skills we teach students. Knowing how to carefully research, evaluate, and interrelate various disciplines matters more than choosing limited, specific subjects for study.

There are many essential cognitive processes and skills that enable our children to succeed in life, solve problems, and continually learn. With the development of these skills and abilities, our children can learn about anything on the list above as well as other topics of interest and importance to them. As Steve Pearlman writes in his book *America's Critical Thinking Crisis*, "*No subject* matters one lick if students lack the capacity to *think* about it."[20]

---

20 See Steven J. Pearlman, *America's Critical Thinking Crisis: The Failure and Promise of Education* (2020), https://www.amazon.com/dp/B08LMZD8KD.

Below are twelve essential skills and cognitive abilities that I believe children need in today's world.[21] Students must be able to:

1. Read, write, and communicate effectively.
2. Understand mathematical concepts and statistics and do basic arithmetic.
3. Understand and employ the scientific method.
4. Conduct effective research, evaluate it for accuracy, and analyze data.
5. Think critically, strategically, logically, analytically, scientifically, and creatively.
6. Understand systems and recognize the many intertwining, systemic causes of problems.
7. Develop and implement solutions to interconnected problems without producing unintended negative consequences.
8. Listen to and evaluate multiple perspectives and be able to employ methods for solving conflicts without hostility or violence.
9. Use technology effectively and understand how various algorithms and platforms work in ways that manipulate and silo people, promulgate misinformation, and lead to uncritical thinking.
10. Work both independently and collaboratively.
11. Self-reflect, self-manage, and self-assess.
12. Act with compassion and determine and embrace choices that do the most good and least harm for

---

21 In the Appendix you will find a longer list of solutionary skills, as well as affective qualities, worthy of cultivation and learning.

themselves and others, including other species and the environment.

With identification of the skills and cognitive capacities young people most need in today's world, we can then develop appropriate curricula. We can begin by reexamining what is currently taught, cultivated, and assessed within traditional curricula since we cannot simply add on to an already full plate. Ultimately, it's in the best interests of our children, our societies, and our world to develop curricula, pedagogical approaches, and school cultures that simultaneously:

- Foster affective qualities such as compassion, wonder, responsibility, and integrity.
- Focus on core skills and thinking capacities that will help them navigate, succeed in, and contribute to the world they live in.
- Teach subjects that most agree are essential for today's world.
- Provide an introduction to numerous subjects so students have exposure to the breadth of worthwhile topics and are poised to think in interdisciplinary ways.
- Ensure students have the ability to transfer knowledge and skills from one discipline to another.
- Create space and time to personalize the curriculum and pedagogy so all children have the ability in school to pursue their own interests, concerns, and talents.
- Enable students to express and cultivate their

creativity and develop and maintain physical and mental health.

- Build communities of respect, understanding, perspective-taking, and collaboration.
- Cultivate the ability to think and act in a solutionary manner.

With these skills in mind, let's return to the content areas mentioned in my long list above. Since the acquisition of skills enables students to learn about any subjects of importance or interest, what content rises to the surface as essential for all U.S. students to know? For me, at this moment, the following seem especially important:

- An overview of the history of humankind
- U.S. history, governance, and civics
- History of caste, slavery, racism, anti-Semitism, sexism, and other manifestations of prejudice and oppression and Movements for justice and rights
- Climate science and climate change
- Ecology, Biology, and Psychology
- Media, disinformation, and conspiracy theories
- Sustainable and ethical living in a globalized world
- Logic and epistemology
- Physical and mental health and Nutrition
- Money and economics
- Statistics and probability
- Exposure and access to various arts (poetry, music, drama, dance, visual arts, etc.)

What rises to the top for you?

What constitutes solutionary thinking?

To be solutionaries, students begin by bringing a solutionary *lens* to problems that they notice in the world and study in school. This means they:

- *see* that problems can be solved
- invite the *perspectives* of others
- *focus* on solutions
- *recognize* that problems don't exist in isolation
- *seek* collaboration
- *look* for ways to ensure that no people, animals, or ecosystems are harmed by their solutions

With a solutionary lens in place, they can then cultivate and practice solutionary *thinking*, which is primarily comprised of:

- Critical thinking
- Systems thinking
- Strategic thinking
- Creative thinking

Critical Thinking

Critical thinking lies at the foundation of solutionary thinking. Without discernment and the ability to ascertain what is factual and distinguish misinformation and disinformation from what is true; to reason; to analyze data; and to assess one's own thinking processes, we cannot build the knowledge necessary to solve problems effectively or in a solutionary manner.

What exactly is critical thinking? The Foundation for Critical Thinking defines it as "the intellectually disciplined process of actively and skillfully conceptualizing, applying, analyzing, synthesizing, and/or evaluating information gathered from, or generated by, observation, experience, reflection, reasoning, or communication, as a guide to belief and action."[22] Critical thinking is challenging. Most of us (myself included) are not proficient enough critical thinkers, and educators are rarely prepared to *teach* critical thinking, even though it is foundational for learning.

How do we know what we know? How do we know that our planet is billions of years old? That we are comprised of atoms? That more people died in the 1918–19 influenza pandemic than in World War I? That a mass extinction is underway? That millions of children are currently living and working as slaves? That nonhuman animals experience pain and suffering on modern industrial farms and in testing laboratories?

Few of us have direct evidence to substantiate the above statements. Rather, we rely on research, experts, and journalism we've come to trust. We also rely on the collective involvement of educated people in many and varied fields to corroborate and demonstrate the validity of hypotheses and theories and to accurately report historical facts and current events.

---

22   For more information about critical thinking, see The Foundation for Critical Thinking, "Defining Critical Thinking," n.d., https://www.criticalthinking.org/pages/defining-critical-thinking/766.

Unfortunately, however, we may come to trust illegitimate and highly biased sources of information based on our already established belief systems. To the greatest degree possible, young people need to learn how to find and evaluate evidence and discover what is factual. They also need to learn to endure the discomfort of cognitive dissonance when their beliefs are challenged by contrary evidence. Confronting cognitive dissonance is challenging because we are disinclined to abandon our deepest beliefs no matter how strong the evidence, and often the greater the evidence the deeper we remain attached to our faulty beliefs. It is even more challenging to confront cognitive dissonance in schools for two reasons:

1. In order for young people to learn to think critically about their assumptions and beliefs, it helps to have teachers actively modeling this themselves, yet this is not something that is normally part of a teacher's job description or their training to be educators.

2. If young people become adept at critical thinking they may begin to think differently from their parents, who may not appreciate their children challenging family norms or beliefs. Parental displeasure may translate into criticism of teachers and schools, causing many schools to keep the curriculum as uncontroversial as possible to avoid conflict.

During Barack Obama's tenure as President of the United States, I was invited to a middle school to give a presentation on learning to make choices that do the most good and least harm for oneself and others. During the presentation, students shared their thoughts in response to my question, "What are the biggest problems in the world?" One boy said, "War." My agreeing that war was a problem alarmed the principal, who worried that this assertion would make parents who were veterans, or fighting in Iraq or Afghanistan, angry. (Ironically, it is soldiers and veterans who know better than most that war is a problem.)

It is worth reporting that no parents expressed concern about by my visit to their children's school, and students told the principal that they learned the following:

- Making connections between one's choices and the impact of those choices on others is important.
- Each of us should endeavor to model a message we're proud of.
- Giving of oneself increases one's own joy.

I tell this story because it represents a trend among many school administrators and politicians to discourage teaching and learning that may be perceived as even remotely controversial. For example, in 2015 members of the West Virginia House of Representatives introduced a bill to prohibit the teaching of "social problems, economics, foreign affairs, the United Nations, world government, socialism or communism until basic courses in American state and local geography and history are completed" (HB 2107). If this bill passed, an offending teacher would be charged with a misdemeanor crime and fined. And then fired.

Such legislation should deeply worry us. One can imagine schools teaching the prerequisite courses only in the upper grades of high school, preventing students from ever having class discussions about important global and social issues—even those heavily reported in the news—throughout most of their schooling. What's ironic, and perhaps tragic, is that there are few places better than schools to address and grapple with "social problems, economics, foreign affairs" and any number of issues, controversial or otherwise, relevant to the lives of our children. Schools and teachers can provide one of the best venues for investigation, research, and analysis, with the goal of turning controversial issues into the clay from which students can mold new ideas and develop meaningful solutions to problems that are all too commonly perceived and presented in either/or terms.

In 2021, in response to the racial-justice reckoning following George Floyd's murder, sixteen states are considering or have signed into law bills that would limit the teaching of certain ideas around race and racism. Such legislation has been opposed by the National Education Association and National Council for Social Studies, and many educators are concerned about the chilling effect these laws will have on classroom discussions about such an important issue.

As long as the issues are presented in an age-appropriate manner, and teachers and administrators take great care not to subtly influence students with their own biases, transforming controversy from polarized camps into problem-solving for all is a wonderful challenge for students and offers the potential for real contributions to society. Moreover, if young people are to become solutionaries, they must be permitted to explore and grapple with controversial topics. One of my favorite examples of the power of young people to address the gravest issues of our time is teacher John Hunter's World Peace Game, in which fourth-graders devise solutions to bring about peace.[23]

Key to addressing controversy is the ability to determine what is actually true. Controversial issues often stem from conflicting beliefs about what is factual. This is why learning how to discern facts from conjecture, disinformation, and misinformation must become an essential goal of schooling. To navigate the media—traditional, alternative, right-leaning, left-leaning, and social—in which any opinion, perspective, pseudo-scientific statement, illegitimate conspiracy theory, etc., vies with valid research, careful journalism, real science, and actual conspiracies, children need to become adept critical thinkers able to challenge biases, including their own, everywhere.

When people actively and energetically pursue information and gain knowledge, they often want to share their new perspectives with others. Sometimes they do so with a critical *attitude*, not just critical *thinking*, and when this happens, learning and thinking suffer. It's important to ensure respectful dialogue in classrooms and reinforce good communication and listening skills. Children need to feel that their opinions and beliefs may be expressed openly, and that no one will be marginalized for having unpopular ideas and perspectives. Parents want to know that persuasive

---

23   Watch John Hunter's top-rated March 2011 TED talk, "Teaching with the World Peace Game," https://www.ted.com/talks/ john_hunter_on_the_world_peace_game?language=en.

teachers who have different values or views won't unduly influence their children, and that the classroom will not become a venue for disrespect toward others' beliefs, values, or cultural traditions.

Systems Thinking

Because life in our world—both ecological and societal—is dependent upon interconnected systems, to be a solutionary it is also essential to become a systems thinker, able to identify the interlinking elements that contribute to the challenges we face. Over time, and despite revolutionary and positive innovations and breakthroughs in science, governance, food production, health care, economics, and more, we have developed entrenched, interrelated systems that have caused, and continue to cause, escalating problems. Although many of our most effective, efficient, and powerful systems have brought great opportunities and liberties and have alleviated tremendous suffering and injustices, our current energy, production, transportation, agriculture, political, and economic systems perpetuate many of the challenges and crises before us.

Attempting to solve a problem in isolation may potentially exacerbate other problems inextricably linked through various systems. While it is not easy to take everyone's interests into consideration, it is necessary to do so in order to avoid partial solutions and/or solutions that help one group while harming another. Here are a few examples of solutions embraced in the United States that have helped alleviate one problem while exacerbating others:

- As we have worked to expand our economy in order to create more prosperity for people, we have contributed to more resource depletion and pollution.

- As we have developed systems to increase the production and reduce the cost of food, we have created environmentally destructive agricultural practices; low-wage and migrant farm jobs without worker protections; and confinement operations that are cruel to animals, resource intensive, and highly polluting.

- As we have outsourced production to developing countries to better compete in the marketplace, keep costs low for consumers, and increase company revenues, we have lost the ability to effectively monitor working conditions and ensure that people in other countries who are producing our clothes, food, electronics, etc., are paid a living wage, treated fairly, and work in safety. Moreover, modern supply chains make it difficult to ensure that enslaved people are not used in the production of many of the goods we purchase. Outsourcing has also meant the loss of U.S. jobs.

- As we have tried to ensure that chemicals entering our environment are safe, we have subjected millions of sentient animals to painful toxicity tests in which chemicals are force-fed to them in quantities meant to kill.

Addressing and changing entrenched and interconnected systems is challenging. When an entire society is structured around certain systems (such as centralized energy grids) it is difficult to move from the predominant system (e.g., fossil fuels) to less centralized systems (e.g., solar, tidal, and wind). When structural forms of oppression and prejudice are pervasive across many systems (e.g. education, housing, banking/lending, incarceration, voting), it is difficult to create an equitable society without addressing all the interconnected systems at once.

Thus, to prepare young people to think comprehensively and deeply about interrelated challenges and to solve problems systemically and wisely, we must educate them to make multiple connections and seek answers that do not cause new problems while solving existing problems. Students need to be able to *understand* complex, interconnected systems; *evaluate* them thoughtfully; and *become* systems thinkers and changers.[24]

Strategic Thinking

Critical and systems thinking provide the foundation for deeply understanding a problem and its effects on people, animals, and the environment, as well as for identifying the human and nonhuman stakeholders who are impacted (both negatively and positively) by the problem and the systems that perpetuate it. To move into the problem-solving stage, we need to cultivate and practice strategic thinking. We may come up with many ideas for solving a problem, and some of these ideas will be more strategic than others. Learning to think strategically leads to a greater likelihood of successful implementation of effective solutions.

---

24 You'll find ways to develop systems thinking competency in Part II.

Strategic thinking involves the identification of practical and powerful leverage points where a tactical change can have a far-reaching impact. The more students investigate the causes of problems, the more connections between systems they will uncover. Not only will they discover the ways that societal and ecological systems interconnect and reinforce problems, they will also deepen their understanding of root causes, such as mindsets, belief systems, and psychological factors that have led us to create these systems.

As students learn to identify the most effective strategies for solving problems, they may search for the deepest leverage points—places where a small change could initiate a cascade of positive outcomes. Often, however, the deepest leverage points lie at the root cause level of human psychology and biology that are difficult or unlikely to change. For example, if we want to solve the problem of growing rates of obesity among children, eliminating children's cravings for high-fat, high-calorie foods would potentially have a huge positive impact, but this is an impractical leverage point, even if it would have far-reaching effects. The other extreme—foregoing deep leverage points for easy fixes at the problem level—isn't particularly strategic either. For example, promoting diets to kids who are overweight might seem like a solution to the problem, but we know that dieting is not especially effective.

A more strategic approach to this problem would be to address the *systems* that:

- Permit advertising of unhealthy foods to children.
- Perpetuate the practice of placing high-fat, nutritionally poor foods into the school lunch program.
- Allow tax subsidies for unhealthy foods, such that

they are the least expensive and most accessible foods for parents to purchase.

- Limit access to a variety of affordable fresh vegetables and fruits in low-income neighborhoods.
- Fail to educate parents on the topic of nutrition for their children.

Creative Thinking

Whereas critical thinking usually entails focused analysis and evaluation to ascertain the truth, creative thinking often happens when we are *not* seeking the "right answer"; when we are open to any and all ideas; and when we are in a playful, relaxed state. The creative impulse is a birthright, but all too often, it becomes buried in school.[25] The more the arts—whether visual, written, dramatic, choreographic, improvisational, or musical—are cut from the school day, the less opportunity our children have to tap into the creative force from which inspiration and ideation often flow.

In relation to becoming a solutionary, creative thinking involves addressing problems in an inventive and/or unorthodox manner; generating ideas that no one has thought of; and/or applying knowledge, skills, and processes from one domain to another in a new way. Creative thinking may come into play not only by devising an innovative solution, but also by discovering ideas that already exist but are not being implemented because of entrenched systems

---

25 See one of the most popular TED talks of all time, Sir Ken Robinson's February 2006, "Do Schools Kill Creativity?" https://www.ted.com/talks/ken_robinson_says_schools_kill_creativity?language=en.

that impede their adoption. The creative thinker may develop ideas for transforming those systems to allow an existing solutionary idea to take root.

Both strategic and creative thinking can be practiced individually as well as collectively. Group brainstorms often produce exciting ideas that spark other ideas among members of the team. Refining these ideas can certainly be done solo, but often the most successful approaches come about through collaboration. When schools play a deliberate role in cultivating opportunities for creative thinking to flourish, they not only enliven everyone participating in the educational endeavor, they also prevent the loss of potential solutions to problems from coming to light and being implemented.

While critical, systems, strategic, and creative thinking happen in a nonlinear fashion, they can and do build upon one another sequentially to help people become more successful solutionaries. Without critical thinking at the base, systems thinking becomes challenging. Without critical and systems thinking operating together, strategic thinking may not successfully advance the most solutionary ideas. And without all three, creative thinking may lack the foundation that enables the imagination to consider new ways to advance the best solutions. Thus, the coaching, practice, and cultivation of these types of thinking need to occur throughout schooling if we want to educate a generation of solutionaries.

What are the systems within education in need of change?
There are many systems within schools themselves that we rarely examine as a society, often because we assume a significant amount of wisdom went into their creation.

Below are some common school systems and practices in the United States. As you read each one, ask yourself if this system or practice best helps achieve the goal of educating and preparing students for their futures and enabling them to effectively participate in the creation of a more sustainable and just world.

Should we:

- Divide the core subjects we teach into the four categories of math, science, language arts, and social studies?[26]
- Teach all children essentially the same things, at the same ages, and in the same ways throughout school?
- Divide units of instruction into short, specific, and predictable time periods of approximately 45 minutes?
- Divide days into class periods with no particular relevance to one another?
- Evaluate student learning primarily with standardized tests and grades?
- Assess schools and teachers based on students' standardized test scores?
- Pay for public schools largely through property taxes, which favor children who live in wealthier areas and limit the funds available for children who live in high-poverty areas?

---

26 Finland has abandoned this system of teaching discrete subjects. See Penny Spiller's May 29, 2017 report for the BBC, "Could Subjects Soon Be a Thing of the Past?" https://www.bbc.com/news/world-europe-39889523.

- Conduct school Monday–Friday, starting around 8 a.m. and ending around 3 p.m. and taking summers off?
- Learn almost exclusively within the walls of the school building,[27] with field trips as a rare treat often distinct from the curriculum, and internship/mentorship opportunities uncommon?
- Avoid democracy in the school as an organizing, decision-making principle worth modeling and practicing?

These pervasive systems and practices have been in place for a long time, and each one deserves reexamination if we are to best educate young people for their important roles and responsibilities in today's world. The next section of this book offers ideas to propel us toward new systems and ways of teaching that will be more relevant and meaningful for children and better prepare them for their futures.

The good news is that many schools, teachers, administrators, curriculum and instructional designers, and parents are transforming schools in their communities and creating innovative programs and approaches. These initiatives, however, are generally not recognized as models worthy of large-scale replication at any level of state or federal government. Additionally, teachers who are dedicated to educating their students to be real-world problem-solvers are

---

27 Although COVID-19 has been tragic for many children who became largely or entirely disenfranchised due to school closures, remote learning during the pandemic also engendered valuable insights and important conversations that may ultimately lead to positive transformations in schools.

often focused on a single concern, rather than on ensuring that their students are educated and prepared to find answers that are good for all people, all species, and the ecosystems that sustain everyone. School reforms are myriad, but not necessarily comprehensive in their nature and vision. That is why it is time to imagine and develop curricula, pedagogical approaches, and schools that simultaneously serve the needs of individual students while enabling them to be contributors to a thriving future for all life.

PART II

EDUCATING YOUNG PEOPLE TO BE SOLUTIONARIES

Begin with yourself.

Educating others to be solutionaries begins with educators cultivating solutionary dispositions within themselves and practicing solutionary skills. We wouldn't teach math without proficiency in math; history without knowledge of history; or science without understanding the sciences. Because the goal of this book is to help people educate others to be solutionaries, it's important for educators to practice along the way in order to develop some personal expertise.

A solutionary is not just a problem-solver. A solutionary is someone who actively:

- Identifies unsustainable, inhumane, and unjust systems.
- Develops and implements systems-based solutions that do the most good and least harm for all people, animals, and the environment.
- Strives to make compassionate and responsible

choices and to support equitable, humane, healthy systems.

The last bullet sets the bar for being solutionary pretty high, given that we cannot easily disentangle ourselves from systems that are unjust toward people, cruel to animals, and environmentally destructive. *But we can try.* To the best of our ability we can examine our choices and work to model a message of kindness, compassion, and responsibility toward others, including other species, through our everyday choices and acts of citizenship. We can cultivate a willingness to learn without defensiveness, introspect about the impacts of our choices, and move in the direction of greater accountability for our decisions.[1]

The first and second bullets bookend the **solutionary process**. You'll find an abbreviated version of this process (which is described fully in the Institute for Humane Education's free digital *Solutionary Guidebook*[2]) in the Appendix of this book. I invite you to choose a problem of concern to you and then go through this process. In doing so, you'll hone your own solutionary thinking and be better prepared to guide others. Chances are that you'll also feel empowered, energized, and enthusiastic about the potential for creating a healthier and more just future, which leads me to another important goal. . . .

---

1   My book *Most Good, Least Harm: A Simple Principle for a Better World and Meaningful Life* (New York: Atria, 2009) describes the keys to do this.

2   Download the guidebook here: https://humaneeducation.org/ solutionary-hub/educate-solutionary-generation/solutionary-guidebook.

Let's teach children that a just, healthy, and peaceful world is possible.

A couple of years ago I led a professional development workshop for educators at a public math and science academy for 10th–12th graders. I began the workshop by asking the group to respond to this prompt: *In 50 years, I want the world to be. . . .* The first teacher to raise her hand said, "still here." When asked whether others shared this feeling, almost all the teachers and curriculum developers raised their hands. Most of them did not feel hopeful about the future.

How might a sense of hopelessness impact teaching, learning, educational goals, and educational outcomes? While hope is not a prerequisite for solutionary thinking and action, without hope it may take a special kind of discipline and integrity to forge a solutionary practice. After all, why bother to work hard at solving entrenched problems if we don't believe they can be solved?

It's not just teachers who are feeling hopeless. In 2012, I spoke to a group of fifth and sixth graders at an independent school in Connecticut. The children shared a list of global challenges, which I wrote down on a white board.[3] I asked them to raise their hands if they could imagine us solving the problems they named. Of the approximately 45 children in the room, only a handful raised their hands. This was one of

---

3   The list generated by these children was quite similar to lists generated by older students and adults, so while I believe it's important to protect young children from the ills of the world, the reality is that even ten-year-olds know about grave global problems without having been taught about them in school.

the most disturbing moments in my career as an educator. I thought to myself, "If these children can't even imagine us solving our problems, what will motivate them to try?"[4]

I knew I had to do something to bring these children some hope, so I asked them to close their eyes, sit comfortably, take some deep breaths, and imagine that they were very old, approaching the end of a long and well-lived life. I described a healthy and humane future, painting a vivid picture of clean air and water, and a world without war, poverty, or oppression of people or animals. It was a similar picture to the one that begins this book. Then I asked them to imagine a child approaching them. This child has been studying history in school and wants to understand how the world has improved so significantly. The child asks this question: "What role did you play in helping to bring about our better world?"[5] I ended the visualization by inviting the students to mentally answer the child's question. With their eyes still closed, I then asked them to raise their hands if now they could imagine us solving our problems. This time, only a handful didn't raise their hands. This suggested that despondency and cynicism might not run very deep, and that the belief in the power to create a brighter future might lie just below the surface if awakened and supported.

With that said, depression and suicide among young people have been on the rise for years. It is our responsibility

---

4   I could understand this widespread hopeless response more if these children were subject to significant hardship and oppression, but these were children in a private school in an affluent community.

5   I've modified this visualization from one originated by deep ecologist, activist, and educator, Joanna Macy.

as teachers, parents, grandparents, mentors, and advocates for a more peaceful world to cultivate practical hope and evidence-based optimism among young people and to engage and support them in meaningful efforts for positive change.[6] This is critically important both for them and the world.

In 2016 I spoke to a group of fifth graders in Guadalajara, Mexico. As I had done in the school in Connecticut, I asked these children if they could imagine us solving the problems we face in the world. Immediately, every hand rose. What was different between these groups of children? The primary difference that I noticed was what and how they were being taught in school. The teacher in Mexico was teaching her students about environmental problems, in age-appropriate ways, and engaging them in efforts to solve them. With the children's involvement, the school had installed solar panels, created a composting system for their cafeteria waste, and replaced individual plastic bottles of water with large purified water jugs from which students refilled their reusable bottles. They were also working on issues beyond their school walls. These children understood that problems could be solved because they had experience solving problems.

---

6   For those children suffering abuse, poverty, and/or oppression, the imperative is to first help these children directly, rather than focus on convincing them that they should be hopeful and optimistic. Then, teachers can endeavor to engage these children in collaborative problem-solving to create positive changes that will relieve their own suffering and address the problems that harm them. This is empowering, helpful work for children to conduct in school as long as it is done in age-appropriate and sensitive ways.

Believing that a better future is possible strengthens hope. Hope then becomes a motivator for action. Action then leads to greater hope, creating a powerful positive feedback loop. Singer-songwriter Joan Baez once said, "Action is the antidote to despair." Professor David Orr phrased the concept this way: "Hope is a verb with its sleeves rolled up." And Greta Thunberg, the Swedish climate activist who received international attention at age thirteen, said in her TEDx talk, "Once we start to act, hope is everywhere."

We have much environmental damage to repair and many systems to transform to create a humane and healthy world for all. The work ahead may seem overwhelming at times, yet it is doable. I'd like to think that if we educate a generation of solutionaries, it will be inevitable. To inspire the greatest number of solutionaries, however, and to improve the likelihood of success, we must commit to ensuring that students *believe* a just, humane, and healthy world is possible and model this message for them through our own participation in citizenship and change-making. If we begin the educational endeavor with this premise, our children will have every reason to engage enthusiastically and fully in the exciting, hopeful, and meaningful work ahead of them. In the process, they will come to know, deep in their hearts and minds, that what they do matters. As young people participate collaboratively and successfully in creating positive change, they will also likely feel the joy and enthusiasm that accompany being part of something larger than themselves and making a meaningful contribution. It is my great hope that we will then see depression and suicide among youth decline.

Let's ensure students understand we are all inextricably connected, and each responsible for the effects of our choices and our collective future.

In his 1963 "Letter from Birmingham Jail," Martin Luther King, Jr. wrote, "We are caught in an inescapable network of mutuality, tied in a single garment of destiny." While specifically written about racial justice, this statement is true of all interconnected systems. Our societal decisions can have negative consequences if we carelessly ignore our "network of mutuality."

For example:

- In 2008, we saw predatory subprime mortgage loans issued in the U.S. to people who couldn't afford them, and then bundled into tradable commodities, bring down economies across the globe.
- In late 2019, a pandemic that originated in China spread to every country in just a couple of months, killing three million people in 16 months.
- Greenhouse gasses emitted into the atmosphere by the U.S., China, and other high fossil fuel–consuming countries are leading to rising sea levels that threaten coastal cities and island nations across the planet.
- Growing resistance by bacteria to antibiotics, caused by both indiscriminate use of these medicines in animals raised for food and excessive and inappropriate prescriptions, now endangers the health of people everywhere.

While intention matters—and only a small percentage of people *intend* to harm others—our choices may cause suffering and destruction whether we are aware of our impacts or not. This is why it is so important that schools teach students to become cognizant of our interconnected lives and the responsibility we share for the effects of our decisions. It really isn't enough to teach our children only to be *proximally* kind (kind to those with whom they interact directly); in today's world it is also important to teach our children (and to learn ourselves) how to be kind through *all* of our choices and to strive for justice for everyone.

To demonstrate how we might teach students to perceive connections and think with systems in mind, I offer you **True Price**, a solutionary-focused activity that develops critical and systems thinking, and which can be adapted to fit a variety of school subjects (including language arts, science, math, and social studies).[7] It can serve as the foundation for a course, unit, or project and can even become the core of an interdisciplinary program. In **True Price**, students ask the following questions about an everyday item (e.g., an article of clothing, an electronic device, a food or beverage, etc.)"

1. What are the effects of this item, both positive and negative, on me, other people, animals, and the environment?
2. What are the societal systems that support, promote, and perpetuate this item? (e.g. economic, produc-

---

7   Download the True Price activity here: https://humaneeducation. org/resources/2013/true-price.

tion, transportation, political, energy, healthcare, agriculture, education, advertising/media, etc.)

3. What alternative products would do more good and less harm for me, other people, animals, and the environment?

4. What systems would need to change, and in what ways, to make alternative products the norm, and what solutionary actions might I take to create such systemic changes?

Below, I demonstrate this activity with an item that is common in most industrialized countries: a fast-food burger. As you will see, I only scratch the surface responding to these **True Price** questions because answering them is a lengthy process that involves research and investigation. My goal in sharing the process of asking and beginning to answer these questions is to provide an example of how students can learn to understand the ways in which everyday choices are connected to ecological and societal systems, as well as how to foster students' compassion and sense of responsibility for the impacts of those choices and systems.

True Price Example: Fast Food Burger
What are the effects, both positive and negative, of a fast-food burger on me, other people, animals, and the environment?
The positive effects of fast-food burgers are obvious, and students do not have trouble articulating them. At the point of purchase, fast-food burgers are inexpensive and filling, as well as tasty and convenient. Their production has spread widely, creating jobs for and increasing the wealth of millions

of people, including those whose retirement funds (whether they know it or not) are invested in fast-food businesses.

Fast-food burgers are also:

- **Unhealthy:** They are high in saturated fats, sodium, cholesterol, calories, and sometimes chemical residues, and low in fiber. Convincing evidence indicates that, eaten frequently, their consumption may lead to heart disease, stroke, weight gain and obesity, type 2 diabetes, and some cancers.[8]
- **Environmentally destructive and wasteful:** According to a 2006 United Nations Food and Agriculture report, meat production is a greater contributor to climate change than either transportation or industry,[9] and recent studies reveal that it may be impossible to reduce global emissions sufficiently unless we change our agriculture system.[10] Meat

---

8   For an overview, see Mark Bitman's "The True Cost of a Burger," *New York Times*, July 16, 2014, http://www.nytimes.com/2014/07/16/opinion/the-true-cost-of-a-burger.html.

9   See Nathan Fiala, "How Meat Contributes to Global Warming," *Scientific American*, February 2009, http://www.scientificamerican.com/article/the-greenhouse-hamburger. Also see the 2010 United Nations Environment Program's report, *Assessing the Environmental Impacts of Consumption and Production*, https://www.resourcepanel.org/reports/assessing-environmental-impacts-consumption-and-production, which recommends a plant-based diet.

10   See Michael A. Clark, Nina G. G. Domingo, Kimberly Colgan, et al. "Global Food System Emissions Could Preclude Achieving the 1.5° and 2°C Climate Change Targets," *Science* 370(6517), November 6, 2020, https://science.sciencemag.org/content/370/6517/705.

production also causes significant pollution in the form of manure and runoff from pesticide- and fertilizer-sprayed feed crops, and requires vastly more land, water, and fossil fuels than plant-based protein sources.

- **Inhumane:** Much ground beef comes from dairy cows who are no longer able to produce milk. Having been annually impregnated, and their young removed within a day so we can take their milk, these cows are forced to produce five to ten times the amount of milk they would naturally produce, often causing mastitis and other ailments, necessitating antibiotics in their feed. Depleted after several years and often lame, these cows are then sent to slaughterhouses, where processing lines move so fast that some cows are not even rendered unconscious before they are hoisted upside down by their legs, and their throats are slit. Slaughterhouse work is also often inhumane toward employees. Not only are the working conditions dangerous, many workers are undocumented laborers without health insurance or recourse when their human rights are violated.

What are the societal systems that support, promote, and perpetuate fast-food burgers? Because of the ways various systems operate (e.g., energy, agriculture, politics, economics, transportation, advertising, etc.), fast-food burgers are ubiquitous despite the problems they cause. Their low price at point of purchase does not reflect their true cost, which is hidden. Government subsidies—made possible through industry lobbying and campaign contributions that exert influence on legislators—result in the use of tax dollars that prevent the full costs of feed-production, water use, land for grazing, transportation, and use of fossil fuels, to be reflected in the price the consumer pays for the burger.[11] The health consequences are also absorbed by tax dollars and by the high costs of health insurance that we all pay. Were it not for these subsidies, fast-food burgers would be quite expensive. Even our legal system, in which disparaging meat is a crime in a number of states, promotes fast-food burgers.[12]

What alternative products would do more good and less harm for me, other people, animals, and the environment? It is easy to come up with personal alternatives to a fast-food burger,[13] and students do so all the time. They often suggest eating a plant-based burger from a company committed to social justice, or a burger from grass-fed cows at organic family farms as alternatives that do more good and less harm.

What systems would need to change, and in what ways, to make alternative products the norm, and what solutionary actions might I take to create such systemic changes? This

---

11   This is why an organic apple may cost the same amount as a burger, the question Kiara was addressing in the Introduction.

12   See: Wikipedia, "Food Libel Laws," n.d., https://en.wikipedia.org/wiki/Food_libel_laws.

13   Although it's not hard to identify more humane, sustainable, and healthy alternatives to fast food, this question can be extremely challenging when other items—such as electronics—are used in **True Price**, because there are no truly sustainable, humane, and just computers or cell phones. This is why the focus on shifting systems is essential.

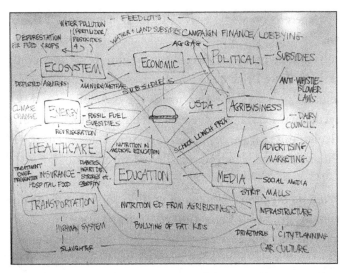

question is the crux of solutionary thinking and action because addressing the systems that would need to change to make healthy, humane, convenient, and affordable food the norm for everyone is challenging. When identifying such systems, students mention those above and many more. They learn how to complete a "mind map" (see above) in which radiating lines from a drawing of a burger connect multiple systems.

Since political, economic, legal, corporate, advertising, energy, transportation, tax subsidy, healthcare, education, agribusiness, city planning, and other societal systems are all connected to fast food, how can students determine truly solutionary ideas to transform these many interconnected systems? Where are the points of leverage that might make an actual systemic impact? [14]

---

14 The Institute for Humane Education's free digital Solutionary Guidebook addresses the problem of growing rates of type

There is no single answer to these questions. If there were, we might have already transformed these systems and solved these problems. To delve further into the answer to this last **True Price** question about system changes, I offer another question, one that forms the basis of a six-week, secondary school, systems- and solutionary-focused curricular unit that we developed at the Institute for Humane Education (and which you can download and use):[15]

What do the primary causes of death in the U.S. have to do with the dead zone in the Gulf of Mexico?[16] It is easy to find information about the causes of the dead zone in the Gulf of Mexico. It is also easy to find information about the primary causes of death in the U.S. Discovering causal connections among the many interconnected systems that contribute to both problems requires committed investigation, research, and analysis. Below is a brief overview of this process.

When students do some research, they discover that the dead zone in the Gulf of Mexico is located where the Mississippi River empties into the ocean. Because of high nitrogen and phosphorus pollution, largely caused by

---

2 "adult-onset" diabetes among children to illustrate the solutionary process, and the sections on leverage points and "solutionary solutions" provide ideas and approaches to answer these questions.

15 Download the unit here: https://humaneeducation.org/resources/2016/primary-death-dead-zone-gulf-mexico-a-solutionary-unit.

16 This question is a modification of one posed by Oberlin College professor David Orr in his book *Earth in Mind: On Education, the Environment, and the Human Prospect* (Washington, D.C.: Island Press, 2004).

agricultural runoff (and to a lesser degree treated sewage), oxygen is depleted in the ocean, leading to hypoxic areas that cannot support life. The dead zone in the Gulf of Mexico grows and declines annually depending upon the weather: droughts in the states along the Mississippi River reduce the area of the dead zone, while floods increase it.

A little more research reveals numerous systems that contribute to nitrogen and phosphorus pollution in the Mississippi River, including the following:

- **Monoculture agriculture** that utilizes nitrogen- and phosphorus-based fertilizers.
- **Concentrated Animal Feeding Operations (CAFOs)**, which require the production of massive amounts of feed crops to be fed to animals. These feed crops, often produced in states with waterways that empty into the Mississippi River, use vastly more fertilizer because of the poor conversion rate of grain to meat than crops grown directly for human consumption.
- **Advertising**, which favors the marketing of highly processed, fertilizer-intensive fast foods and junk foods over organically produced plant foods for direct consumption, such as legumes, grains, nuts, and fresh fruits and vegetables.
- **Political and energy systems** that support ethanol production, which relies upon nitrogen- and phosphorus-based fertilizers used in corn production.[17]

---

17 Ethanol production seemed like a good idea when it was

- **Economic and legal systems** that extend First Amendment freedoms to corporations, thus allowing companies and their lobbyists to influence legislators through campaign contributions that result in all of the above, along with tax subsidies that keep environmentally destructive and energy-intensive foods inexpensive at the point of purchase.

When students research the primary causes of death among people in the U.S., they discover that number one is heart disease, followed closely by cancer. Numbers five and seven are stroke and diabetes respectively.[18] They learn that diet is one of the leading contributors to heart

---

introduced as a fuel option. It diminished dependence on fossil fuels and offered an alternative to the unpredictable global oil market. By becoming more self-sufficient and using a renewable resource, the U.S. hoped to produce energy, reduce reliance on foreign oil, and make an environmentally sustainable choice. But ethanol production comes with negative effects, including nitrogen- and phosphorus-based fertilizer runoff and the conversion of forests to corn production, which increases greenhouse gas emissions by reducing the carbon sink that forests provide. Many scientists have now concluded that when all connected systems are examined closely, ethanol production actually *increases* rather than decreases total greenhouse gases, the opposite effect from its intended use (see University of Berkeley, California. "Ethanol Production Consumes Six Units of Energy to Produce Just One," *Science Daily*, April 1, 2005, http://www.sciencedaily.com/releases/2005/03/050329132436.htm).

18 The figures are from the Centers for Disease Control and Prevention (CDC), 2017: http://www.cdc.gov/nchs/fastats/leading-causes-of-death.htm. Statistics that include the impact of COVID-19 on these numbers are not available as of this writing.

disease, several cancers,[19] stroke, and type 2 "adult-onset" diabetes—which is occurring at an alarming rate among children.[20] With more digging to uncover the systems that contribute to unhealthy diets in the U.S., students learn that many of those systems identified above as contributors to the dead zone in the Gulf of Mexico are also responsible for ill health among people in the U.S., along with other systems including medical education and health care, which often favor treatment of diseases over prevention, and legal, economic, and governmental systems that allow industries to provide nutrition curricula to schools that promote their own products, whether or not they are healthy choices.

The points above only touch upon the systems that connect the dead zone and public health problems. I share them to provide a taste of what problem identification and systems thinking entail (as well as to describe what students will explore if teachers utilize the curricular unit we've created). Once students determine the causes of problems, investigate them fully, research the ways in which they have been addressed by others, and identify the impacts of various approaches, they are then poised to identify solutions that are humane, just, and sustainable for people, other species, and the environment.

---

19   See the World Health Organization International Agency for Research on Cancer, "IARC Monographs Evaluate Consumption of Red Meat and Processed Meat," October 26, 2015, http://www.iarc.fr/en/media-centre/pr/2015/pdfs/pr240_E.pdf.

20   See Centers for Disease Control, "Rates of New Diagnosed Cases of Type 1 and Type 2 Diabetes Continue to Rise Among Children, Teens," n.d., https://www.cdc.gov/diabetes/research/reports/children-diabetes-rates-rise.html.

What might the students' solutionary ideas, work, and outcomes be? Much depends on what the students uncover in their research, and where their individual interests and talents lie. Below are some possibilities. Students might:

- Draft legislation to present to elected officials that offers suggested changes and improvements to energy, campaign financing, advertising, and tax subsidy systems (gaining skills in investigation, writing, civic engagement, and public speaking).

- Address the agriculture system through education, teaching others about healthy, humane, just, and sustainable food production to increase the demand for foods that are good for people and the environment and humane toward animals, and decrease the demand for unhealthy, unsustainable, and inhumane foods (gaining skills in research, advocacy, and communication). Some students might address systems within their own school and work to transform their cafeterias, while others might build an edible school or community garden (gaining skills and knowledge about community-building, design, botany, ecology, soil science, nutrition, and food-production).

- Consult and intern with innovators, scientists, farmers, and professionals who are: building regenerative, just, and sustainable farming systems; developing healthy, affordable, and delicious plant-based proteins as well as cultivated meat from cells; and producing clean, renewable, cost-effective energy options (gaining knowledge and skills in science, math, business, engineering, and innovation).

Looping back to **True Price**, it is the work described above, and the solutions that arise from it, that ultimately provide students with the answers to the fourth **True Price** question about what systems would need to change to make healthy, humane, environmentally sustainable food commonplace.

When students are offered opportunities to analyze their own and society's choices and creatively and collaboratively develop systemic solutions to problems they uncover in their investigations, they gain a deep understanding that we are all inextricably connected, ecologically and societally; they realize their everyday choices have impacts on others; they gain real-life experiences worthwhile for their futures; they are rewarded with the joy that comes from purposeful contribution; and they deepen their sense of responsibility for our collective future. And all this happens while they develop foundational literacy, numeracy, scientific, communication, and critical, systems, strategic, and creative thinking skills.

Let's ensure that students understand how to develop *solutionary* solutions.

If you conduct a web search for "kid heroes" you'll discover children doing wonderful things. It is inspiring to read their stories, learn about their generosity, and know that kindness and compassion flourish.

When I searched for "kids saving the world" and "kid heroes," I found hundreds of stories about what children have contributed. Below are some of them. They may seem familiar, because children do these sorts of things regularly, often as part of school community service initiatives:

- Donated groceries to a food bank.
- Donated blankets to a homeless shelter and an animal shelter.
- Raised money to send livestock to developing countries.
- Raised money to help people recover after a natural disaster.
- Held a rodeo to raise money for a health charity.

These efforts stem from generous hearts, and we should applaud humanitarian acts that do the most good and least harm because they are essential to alleviate immediate suffering. However, it is important to note that none of these efforts address a *system* in need of change, and some inadvertently harm others, especially animals (e.g., the rodeo and providing livestock).

If we ignore the root and systemic causes of problems, we will perpetually be putting out (literal and metaphorical) fires. For example, if we depend upon tax-payer dollars and individual generosity to help people displaced by climate change–caused floods, crop failures, and forest fires, but do not address the systems that lead to climate change, we will need to help those suffering from these less-than-natural disasters in perpetuity. Similarly, if we don't develop systems for people to move out of poverty or correctives for systems that privilege certain groups over others, we will always be faced with the need for aid. And if we cause unintended harm to one group while trying to help another, we simply aren't being solutionary.

Distinguishing between a solution and a *solutionary* solution can be challenging. Often, ideas to solve problems might seem very promising until we analyze them deeply and discover that they may not actually be solutionary. This Solutionary Scale offers a tool for assessing the "solutionariness" of solutions:

EMERGING	DEVELOPING	SOLUTIONARY	MOST SOLUTIONARY
The solution, while well-intentioned, does not yet address rood and/or systemic causes (and may produce unintended negative consequences to people, animals, or the environment).	The solution addresses root and/or systemic causes but produces unintended negative consequences to people, animals, or the environment.	The solution addresses root and/or systemic causes and strives not to produce unintended negative consequences to people, animals, or the environment.	The solution **significantly and strategically** addresses root and/or systemic causes and does not harm people, animals, or the environment.

Using this scale, ask yourself where the following solution falls:

In May 2015, a CNN Hero report highlighted the good work of a young man who wanted to solve the problems of food waste and hunger simultaneously. His idea was to create a nonprofit and utilize the efforts of volunteers to bring food that would otherwise be thrown out by restaurants to hungry people living in poverty. Soon he had built a thriving program with many volunteers transporting food from restaurants to soup kitchens and food pantries.

Is this solution Emerging? Developing? Solutionary? Most Solutionary?

While the solution certainly alleviates some local problems and helps many individuals, does it address or seek to solve the systems that perpetuate hunger and/or the systems that perpetuate food waste? Is it a scalable solution? Would it be feasible for volunteers to transport the excess food produced and wasted into the hands of all people living in hunger? Would it solve the primary cause of hunger, which is poverty and lack of access to affordable, nutritious food?

In 2018, I spoke at a teacher's conference in New York City, and I shared the CNN Hero clip of this man and his volunteers. I asked the audience to rate his solution on the solutionary scale, just as I asked you to do. Most rated it as Emerging or Developing. Interestingly, one of the teachers in the audience was a volunteer at a food pantry that was the recipient of this nonprofit's efforts. I was eager to hear her thoughts from her personal experience. She told us that they sometimes had so much leftover food delivered that they were unable to distribute it and had to dispose of it themselves. Thus, there were times when volunteers were transporting food from restaurants to food pantries, only to have it thrown away by other volunteers. Please understand that I am not suggesting that we stop supporting such initiatives, which are helping hungry people and reducing the disposal of perfectly good food. What I *am* suggesting is that we simultaneously work to devise ever more solutionary solutions to address these issues at the systems level.

Assessing solutions on the solutionary scale is not math. There is rarely one "right answer." Opinions will differ, and teachers should welcome a variety of viewpoints. Some people evaluating the CNN Hero's solution, for example, rate it as Solutionary and offer cogent reasons for their assessment. With that said, the rubric helps us move toward more and better solutionary thinking and action.

Let's make learning interdisciplinary and organized around real-world issues.

In most schools, students study math, science, language arts, and social studies in discrete classes. A student might be learning algebra in math (from a textbook or computer program); studying biology in science (from a different textbook or computer program); reading *Hamlet* in language arts; and exploring European history (from yet another textbook). Every 45 minutes the bell rings, and the student switches gears entirely. There is little continuity, connection, or common thread. Nothing about this typical school model has a counterpart in the working world.

To make schools both solutionary-focused and inter-disciplinary we can organize learning around pressing, real-world challenges. Using current overarching issues as keystones will enable many schools that may not be able to easily or quickly change their current course structure to integrate otherwise discrete disciplines through the lens of a relevant theme. Below is an example of how the real-world challenge of **climate change** could fit into the current structure of most schools, making the curriculum more pertinent, interdisciplinary, and solutionary.

Students could learn topics in science by studying the greenhouse effect; the changing chemistry of our atmosphere and oceans; the physics of rising sea levels and air currents; the biological impacts on ecosystems; the increasing rates of extinction; the science behind the growing numbers and strength of hurricanes and tropical storms; and the migration of some plant and animal species toward the cooler poles. They might analyze the data produced by approximately 97 percent of climate scientists who conclude that humans are contributing to global warming. They could then offer ideas based on their scientific knowledge for addressing and slowing climate change, adapting to new climate realities, and adopting and advocating personal choices to reduce climate impacts on a school-wide level.

Students could practice and develop their math skills through equations, statistics, and graphing to analyze climate trends; design and conduct quantitative research studies; conduct cost-benefit analyses; quantify the primary causes of increased greenhouse gasses in the atmosphere; and solve climate change–oriented mathematical problems.

They could gain language arts skills by engaging with current writings on climate change; dystopian and utopian literature; American nature-oriented classics like Thoreau's *Walden* and the poetry of George Marion McClellan, as well as modern poetry by Camille Dungy and Mary Oliver. They might write blog posts, op-eds, fiction, poetry, and/or essays sparked by these readings, with the goal of producing publishable written work that has a meaningful real-world impact.

Students could learn about history and geography as they explore the societal impact of droughts, floods, topsoil depletion, desertification, and deforestation on civilizations throughout time and compare these historical impacts with current realities. They would have the opportunity to think critically and strategically about the politics, psychology, and economics involved in climate change, and the various methods and approaches of groups working to reverse the changes we've set in motion, covering topics in social studies.

Some students might explore how and why many people dismiss climate change despite the evidence and the overwhelming scientific consensus and cultivate the ability to respectfully and effectively challenge persistent climate change myths. Other students might examine the ways in which climate change impacts different groups of people, such as those living on island nations, along coasts, and in regions that are becoming more desertified, drought-prone, fire-prone, and/or flood-prone; those enduring poverty; and those who are subject to oppressive systems connected to caste, ethnicity, religion, and race that may limit where they can live and the opportunities available to them to avoid the worst of climate change's impacts.

Students' solutionary work in this realm could include:

- preparing and meeting with policy-makers to present their suggestions;
- creating educational presentations to share with the greater community;
- creating design solutions, videos, and thought-provoking, inspiring spoken word/poetry and/or dramatic productions;
- bringing their social studies analyses to a wider audience through shareable and publishable work;
- working within their own school to transform its energy and/or food systems to reduce its carbon footprint.

This last example of identifying and solving problems in their own school is a reminder that students do not need to be tasked with solving the problem of climate change on a global scale. They can address a local manifestation of this bigger problem, and their solutions can then be spread, scaled up, and become systemic, ultimately having a hugely positive impact.

* * *

Here is an interdisciplinary idea for meaningful curricula across all grade levels that could have a positive impact on both individual students and the larger school-wide community: once a year, an entire school district could address the same topic for a four- to six-week block of time. Let's take the topic of **energy** as an example. While young students might be learning about energy in their own bodies, calories in food, and healthy eating for optimum energy, middle school students might be studying renewable energy sources and comparing them to coal and other fossil fuels, learning about geography, politics, economics, and science, and using math and probabilities. Older students might learn from scientists and engineers who are developing clean and sustainable energy systems, as well as from community organizers working to build a green economy that provides well-paying jobs to people who've been historically marginalized due to race or ethnicity. They might then conduct independent research with the goal of drafting proposed energy and community solutions.[21]

---

21   Some of the older students might pursue a Solutionary Career

The final week of the study of each real-world topic could be set aside for celebrations of learning during which students share with both the school and greater community the knowledge gained, problems identified, and solutions achieved. Imagine the learning and doing (and learning by doing) that would take place; the engagement and motivation that would be inspired by the students' passion about a particular issue or problem; the community involvement that would enrich the students' investigations and projects; and the excitement of seeing the ways in which what happens in school relates to what happens in the real world when an overarching topic provides the focal point. And imagine the rich dimensions of such topical study! Here are just a few examples of potential topics:

Things we can't live without:
- Food and water
- Energy, transportation, and shelter
- Clothing and essential products

Persistent problems in the world:
- Pollution, resource depletion, and habitat destruction
- Sexism, racism, and other forms of discrimination
- Violence, poverty, human trafficking, war

Certification (described in the Appendix) in solar design and installation inspired by such a program.

Creating positive change:
- Conflict resolution and peacemaking
- Ethical choice-making and effective change-making
- Regenerative and just systems development

To understand and meaningfully address these topics, students would necessarily build their knowledge of and skills in the sciences and math, learn about history and current events, and practice oral and written communication. Moreover, to make an impact, students would gain leadership, goal setting, and the critical, systems, strategic, and creative thinking capacities mentioned earlier. They would likely find themselves striving to live with greater compassion, integrity, and responsibility as well.

Here is another idea: what if we had **solutionary-focused questions** that guided curriculum development throughout K–12 schooling; that were connected to skill and knowledge acquisition; and that covered the truly essential needs of our lives? Here are some:

- *How can the systems in our world work effectively, ethically, and sustainably?*
- *How does positive change happen?*
- *How can we be solutionaries for a just, peaceful, and sustainable world for all people, other species, and the environment?*

Now imagine that from each overarching question come more questions that serve as topics within developmentally appropriate units. Below are some examples.

As you read them, consider what ages the question is best suited for, what disciplines connect to the question, and what transferable understandings might be gained while exploring the answers.

From the question, *How can the systems in our world work effectively, ethically, and sustainably?* classes might explore answers to the following questions:

- *What are ecological and societal systems, and how do they connect?*
- *On what societal and ecological systems do we depend?*
- *What are the impacts on a system from decisions made in another system?*

From the question, *How does positive change happen?* students might ask and answer these questions:

- *How do ideas develop and spread?*
- *In what ways are technologies transforming our capacity to create positive change, and in what ways are they hindering our positive impact?*
- *What kinds of advocacy and activism most readily change societies for the better and what kinds often or sometimes backfire?*

From the question, *How can we be solutionaries for a just, humane, and sustainable world for all people, other species, and the environment?* students could explore these questions:

- *What are my deepest values, and how can I live accordingly in a globalized world?*
- *What does it mean to be a solutionary* _____ ?
  (Fill in the blank with any profession or job.)
- *How can we each best model our message and do the most good and least harm for ourselves and others, including nonhuman animals and the environment?*[22]

While schools and teachers might offer some or all of these questions to students within units of study, equally important is eliciting students' own questions, some of which might become a topic for the class, and others of which might become the students' personal quests that they turn into projects, challenges, and their own solutionary work and accomplishments.

Allowing room in the day and within the curriculum for teachers to collaborate in an interdisciplinary manner in order to address current issues that affect students will make learning truly relevant and engaging. When the 9/11 attacks happened in 2001, how many teachers in secondary schools in the U.S. were given the support, guidance, and trust to pause and alter the curriculum so that students could confront, make sense of, and grapple with the gravity of what had befallen their country and fellow citizens? Certainly, there was discussion *in retrospect* about how this *should* have happened, but did much change over the next two decades? Were teachers encouraged to shift the

---

22   Mahatma Gandhi was once asked by a reporter, "What is your message?" He responded, "My life is my message." This is true for all of us, hence this question.

focus of their curricula when Hurricane Katrina struck the Gulf states of the U.S. in 2005, or when Hurricane Sandy devastated the coast of the mid-Atlantic states in 2012?

In 2020–2021, when crises piled up one after the other, did teachers have enough experience and tools, and were they permitted to shift their curricula toward urgent lessons related to:

- **pandemics**—given that students were living through COVID-19, the worst pandemic in a century?
- **climate change**—given that the most extensive and destructive wildfires in our lifetimes occurred in Australia and the west coast of the United States?
- **racism**—given that tens of thousands of people in the U.S. and beyond took to the streets to protest anti-Black racism after the killing of George Floyd under the knee of a police officer?
- **media literacy**—given that disinformation and misinformation were on the rise, and conspiracy theories were gaining ever more traction and followers?
- **conflict resolution and solutionary thinking**— given that political polarization in the U.S. rose to new and ever more contentious levels to the point that our democracy was threatened?

Learning how to create collaborative, meaningful, and responsive interdisciplinary curricula is essential for schooling that prepares students for the real world, and the process can be deeply creative and exciting for teachers, as long as they are given time, training, tools, resources, support, and trust.

I realize that some of these ideas require rethinking the current structure of typical courses and curriculum, which isn't easy to do within large public-school systems. Yet, if we don't assess and evaluate our current systems in light of an ever-evolving, opportunity-rich world, we will ultimately thwart children's learning, diminish their engagement with their studies, and leave them poorly prepared for their future.

Let's prepare students to be solutionaries through varied pedagogical approaches.

While curriculum is the body of knowledge, subjects, and skill sets that are presented to students, pedagogy is the *method* of that transmission. We are all familiar with the "sage on the stage" model of delivery, in which the teacher stands at the head of the classroom, in front of a board or screen, and speaks to the students who are sitting—usually in rows—at desks. Sometimes this method is useful. When people have important knowledge and information to share, it makes sense for them to share it. The popularity of TED talks is a testament to the value of the sage-on-the-stage teaching; however, this pedagogical approach should be delivered only in small doses.

There are so many other ways in which children can acquire information that leads to knowledge, and skills that lead to real-world solutionary accomplishments. Below are a few different pedagogical approaches offered as examples to serve a curricular unit around the question, ***How can we ensure that everyone has access to clean water?*** Let's assume that the goals for this unit are that students will obtain skills in and motivation for:

- Literacy, numeracy, and the scientific method
- Critical, systems, strategic, creative, and design thinking
- Problem finding and problem solving
- Compassion, communication, and collaboration
- Responsibility

Further, let's assume the goals also include gaining some content knowledge within the disciplines of ecology, chemistry, biology, physics, governance, ethics, social studies, history, math and statistics, and geography.

The teacher might utilize a mix of the following pedagogical approaches:

Use inquiry. Elicit students' queries about water as well as pose and discuss such questions as: Who has a right to clean water? Why do approximately 1.5 billion people lack access to safe drinking water? What happens when water sources are privatized? Given that we live in a closed ecological system, where has the freshwater gone? What causes desertification? What is causing the depletion of so many aquifers? How much water does it take to produce bottled water?

Offer opportunities for independent research and investigation. Invite students to identify an aspect of the topic that is of greatest interest to them (e.g., polluted local waterways, contaminated tap water, lack of access to clean water, deforestation and its relationship to desertification and water availability, water privatization, depleted local aquifers, etc.); do independent research; and critically assess the validity and reliability of the research.

Offer experiential opportunities for learning. Have students trace their own water supplies from source to final destination, visit both places, and learn from the people involved in the delivery of fresh water and treatment of sewage. Have some students take samples from local waterways and conduct a chemical analysis of them, while others conduct, analyze, and/or compare chemical tests from both tap and bottled water.

Invite speakers. Invite guests to talk to students by videoconference or in person, such as someone who has grown up without access to a personal well, plumbing, or easily obtainable sources of water; a representative from a corporation that is privatizing water or marketing bottled water; an individual who has invented an inexpensive water treatment device; a scientist who has documented the impact of water pollution and contamination; an expert in water policy, etc.

Use films and other multimedia sources. Have discussions about films that address water issues, from pollution and contamination, to privatization, to lack of access, to the impacts of plastic bottling and transportation of bottled water on the environment.

Use real-life case studies. Provide examples of challenges, successes, partial successes, and failures in addressing access to clean water, so that students can develop their own ideas in a real-world context, understanding what efforts have been made and what obstacles have arisen. Explore personal stories of people impacted by water scarcity and/or contamination—such as children drinking municipal water contaminated by lead—to gain knowledge, deepen understanding and compassion, and inspire solutionary action.

Provide time and mentoring for solutionary work. Give students the time and space to develop their own solutionary approaches or pursue one of the following: ideas for the design or modification of existing water purification, collection, or dissemination devices; a probability diagram showing the expected changes in a body of freshwater if certain social, economic, and political issues are not addressed, and, conversely, if they are addressed successfully, in order to spur positive action; a shareable presentation or video that analyzes water usage for various foods, products, and home and recreational use that offers suggested options to reduce water usage and protect aquifers and freshwater supplies; opportunities for legal recourse against municipalities that knowingly allow lead-contaminated water to harm children.

Offer opportunities for collaborative work. Help students work in groups and teams to develop their solutions through collaboration. Here's an imagined scenario to serve as an example: Aisha is an advanced science student years ahead of her grade level. Justin is an excellent writer with a blog that many fellow students read regularly. Martina loves doing research and is a proficient critical and systems thinker. José is an artist and already very good at graphic design. Kyra is a quintessential diplomat who listens calmly and openly. Working together, they develop a solution to the problem of pollution in their local river and prepare a presentation, utilizing each of their talents, efforts, and knowledge, to share their solution with their community so that it gains widespread support for implementation. On their own, each has much to contribute; together, they are a force.

Let's adopt more meaningful assessments.

Grades and scores on standardized tests are our current measure of learning,[23] yet it's important to ask if these are truly the best ways to evaluate students' understanding, mastery, and achievement, and whether they support solutionary thinking and accomplishments. What exactly do grades and standardized tests measure? How often does a poor grade or test score have more to do with a child being hungry, living in an unsafe situation, experiencing sleep deprivation, enduring bullying, or suffering from discrimination? How

---

23 In October 2015, President Obama disseminated a video that admitted that current standardized testing protocols were not working to achieve their goals. The outcry against frequent high-stakes testing, and the activism that has led families to opt out of them and some states to limit them, is being heard. See Rebecca Mead, "Obama's Change of Heart on Testing," *New Yorker*, October 28, 2015,: http://www.newyorker.com/news/daily-comment/obamas-change-of-heart-on-testing?

often do standardized tests reflect inherent biases related to racial and cultural backgrounds, income, neurodiversity, and other factors that undermine their validity? Do grades and standardized tests motivate students to put in more effort, learn more effectively, retain their learning, and/or produce real-world contributions?[24]

Grades are not simply assessments of learning: when placed on a curve, every test, quiz, exam, and graded assignment is a mini-competition, comparing students to their peers rather than measuring actual achievement and learning.[25] Shouldn't our goal be that 100% of students understand the subjects they're studying and master the skills teachers are cultivating in them? Yet if every student got straight As, some might accuse the school of grade inflation and say that grades no longer had meaning. If our goal is that every child gains proficiency in essential skills and competencies; has exposure to a variety of interconnected disciplines; increases knowledge about content we determine is essential for all; has the necessary capacities to make meaningful contributions to society; and is able to accurately and meaningfully assess their accomplishments, how do grades ensure that this happens?

---

24 We might also ask what we can learn from the cancellation of standardized tests during COVID-19 that can be carried forward post-pandemic.

25 As a teenager, I felt relieved when our math teacher graded on a curve after a difficult test. Motivated by grades, I was happy to get a high grade *in comparison* with my classmates, even if I didn't understand the concepts well enough to master the material and do well without the curve. Only in retrospect did I realize the weakness of this grading model.

As Salman Khan, founder of Khan Academy, has discussed in his widely viewed TED talk, if students get less than 100% on a test of their knowledge and skills (in math, for example) that may mean they didn't fully understand the concepts, and they have gaps that will prevent ultimate mastery. The grading model has a tendency to penalize failure, rather than ensure that students practice until they gain proficiency, as well as to enable students to move to the next level before they are fully ready. Grades also potentially promote complacency because many students may be satisfied with a B even though such a grade means they haven't mastered the content or skill. Grades can then become a ranking system rather than a mastery system.

Without mastery of the building blocks, students have a weak foundation for the acquisition of higher-level knowledge, which can result in both diminished student engagement and failure to understand and advance. Further, by externalizing the reward for learning, children may lose the pleasure and excitement that is a normal response to learning something new. And children who do not get high marks may lose confidence, interest, and motivation in school.

What are some other ways we might assess and evaluate learning? Below are a few assessment strategies that are currently being explored and utilized, and which might be integrated more regularly into all schools:

- Through daily formative assessments of writing, speaking, and calculating, students demonstrate their understanding and ability during class and get the necessary help as soon as a gap in understanding is observed by the teacher or the student.

- Students move ahead based not on time spent on a subject or skill, but rather mastery. Khan Academy operates on this method, and schools could do the same, especially with computer technologies that can automatically record progress and competency-attainments.

- Once a skill or understanding has been mastered, the student teaches another student, demonstrating both mastery and teaching.

- English, history, social studies, and other humanities classes become discussion- and concept-based, with achievement measured by the development of thinking and communication skills. Students' writing is carefully evaluated and improved through one-on-one feedback with teachers and/or writing mentors. An essay, piece of fiction, poem, interview, article, presentation, and/or speech is perfected over time, so that mastery is accomplished and a student's writing or presentation can become worthy of publication or sharing with an authentic audience.

- Students demonstrate learning by doing; they accomplish tasks and achieve goals that are otherwise impossible to attain without specific abilities, skills, and understandings, and which contribute to society (e.g., designing a sustainable and functional structure; identifying and calculating ways to conserve energy in school; writing a cogent, thought-provoking op-ed on an issue in the news, etc.).

- Students' artistic projects—whether visual, dramatic, or spoken word—provide expressive, creative, and innovative examples of conceptual understandings.
- Students form panels of teachers and mentors and invite community members to ask them questions about a topic they've been studying to demonstrate deep understanding and ability to articulate learning.
- Students learn to carefully, critically, and effectively assess themselves and their work. They learn to perceive their strengths, gaps, and weaknesses and to create personal plans—in collaboration with teachers, mentors, and parents—to address gaps and weaknesses while utilizing strengths.

Students assessed in these ways can build a meaningful digital portfolio of accomplishments that demonstrate the body of knowledge and competency acquisition they've obtained (including mastery of subjects from online technologies); showcase their solutionary achievements; and include evaluations of their work and thoughtful narratives from teachers, mentors, and supervisors.

> **Let's offer students self-reflective practices
> to promote healthy states of mind as well as
> positive attitudes and behaviors.**

There are schools that are teaching mindfulness meditation to their students, discovering that it improves attention and helps students to manage stress and cultivate self-control.[26]

---

26 See articles at the Mindfulness in Schools Project: http://

Mindfulness is just one form of meditation during which students learn to observe their thoughts and feelings without reacting to them. In passage meditation,[27] students choose and memorize values-rich, inspiring writing, repeating these memorized passages in their mind to cultivate and deepen qualities that represent wisdom, good character, and ethics.

Naikan, a Japanese form of self-reflection, is another introspective practice that often leads people toward the experience of gratitude and the desire to be kinder, more patient, and more responsible for their actions. Practitioners ask and answer three questions:

1. What have I received from _____?
2. What have I given _____?
3. What troubles or difficulties have I caused _____?

Filling in the blank with individuals (peers, family members, teachers, those far removed but connected through the global economy, etc.); aspects of nature (air, water, soil, forests, etc.); other species (companion animals, wildlife, farmed animals, animals in laboratories, animals used for entertainment, etc.), or simply filling in the blank with "today," allows students (and teachers) to take stock of their reality; become cognizant of the myriad contributors

---

mindfulnessinschools.org/research/research-evidence-mindfulness-young-people-general.

27 Passage meditation was brought to the U.S. by India-born teacher Eknath Easwaran, a professor of literature at the University of California at Berkeley.

to all that they may otherwise take for granted; become more aware of their impacts on others; introspect from an observational, informed perspective; evaluate their choices; and hold themselves accountable.[28]

These and other forms of self-reflection and meditation invite students to become more self-aware, peaceful, and composed; to develop equanimity; to cultivate positive character traits; and to practice self-assessment. With self-reflection also comes a greater capacity for healthy, positive, compassionate communication, which leads to better conflict resolution, restorative practices, and the ability to collaborate more effectively to solve problems.

It's important to note that for students who are experiencing hunger, abuse, prejudice, bullying, or other traumatic circumstances, these generally positive self-reflective practices may not be particularly helpful and could even be harmful if we do not, first and foremost, help to ensure that their basic physical and emotional needs are met.[29]

Let's commit to students' physical health and fitness.
Despite our tremendous achievements in medicine and health care, our children are growing heavier, less fit, and

---

28   For more information about *Naikan* practice see *Naikan: Gratitude, Grace and the Art of Self Reflection* by Gregg Krech (Berkeley, CA: Stone Bridge Press, 2001).

29   For ideas about how to support children impacted by trauma see Lea Waters and Tom Brunzell, "Five Ways to Support Students Affected by Trauma," *Greater Good Magazine*, August 13, 2018, https://greatergood.berkeley.edu/article/item/five_ways_to_ support_students_affected_by_trauma.

less healthy. The systems that are perpetuating this trend are complex and interconnected. This book has already touched upon a few of them in the **True Price** example of fast-food burgers and the curricular question about the connection between the primary causes of death in the U.S. and the dead zone in the Gulf of Mexico. As previously mentioned, our agricultural, economic, political, advertising, and other systems are all contributors to public health issues.

Schools simply must become places where healthy food is the norm. While some states, schools, and districts are moving in a positive direction regarding the healthfulness of foods and beverages provided to children in schools, cafeterias are a primary place where the USDA distributes unhealthy, high-fat, high-sodium, low-fiber foods.[30] In many schools, vending machines still churn out sugary drinks—whether juice or sugar-sweetened beverages—and junk food. By transforming school cafeterias, we not only help children stay healthy and develop lifelong healthful eating habits, but also model just, humane, and sustainable food choices. Many students already note the discrepancy between what they are learning in health classes about nutrition and much of what is available in the cafeteria.

Some schools are building indoor, rooftop, and outdoor gardens and greenhouses and are integrating them into the life science and health curriculum, as well as the cafeteria, providing examples for other districts to follow. Such programs provide excellent opportunities for learning

---

30 Investigating why this is the norm provides another excellent opportunity for systems thinking.

about sustainable food production and scientific subjects while producing healthy food directly for the school.

Let's also revitalize physical education (PE). Imagine if all students were offered a variety of PE opportunities that serve body *and mind*, such as yoga, Aikido, a range of dance forms, strength and high intensity interval training (HIIT), etc. With time to sample and experience each, students could choose one or two as a regular practice, learning discipline and mastering a mind–body form that would serve them throughout their lives. Each of these practices has benefits that extend beyond fitness. Aikido is a martial art that turns aggression into nonviolent resolution—a bodily practice of one of the most important skills we must cultivate for a peaceful world. Dance is physically rigorous and offers opportunities for creative expression, improvisation, and collaboration. Yoga builds strength, flexibility, focus, and inner calm, and may be more suited for those who wish to participate in non-contact activities and/or who need or want a more meditative practice. Strength training and HIIT require as much mental as physical discipline and build bone and muscle mass, endurance, and stamina, which can carry forward into the rest of students' lives, paving the way for long term fitness and health. Let's also make sure to provide opportunities for children with various levels of ability and disability so that no one is left out.

There are, of course, team sports that offer young people excellent opportunities not only for fitness but also to learn teamwork and sportsmanship, and they can be very positive activities physically, socially, and mentally. As children grow up, however, teams become ever more selective and competitive, resulting in physical outlets for some, while leaving others with few opportunities, other than the occasional gym class, for any physical activities during the school day. And for those children with disabilities, team sports may exclude them entirely.

In Finland, acclaimed for its superb educational system, team sports are optional community activities and have nothing to do with schools. Knowing that other countries organize sports differently may encourage U.S. schools to put team sports in a wider and wiser context. Right now, successful school athletes and top teams are venerated out of proportion to non-athletic pursuits.

As one example, about a decade ago I was at a community theater production, and during the closing scene at around 11 p.m., a fire siren started sounding by the high school right outside the theater for several minutes. Finally the siren stopped, just as the show came to an end. I turned to the person next to me, who was less alarmed than I. Having grown up in this town, he correctly surmised that the sirens were announcing a win for the basketball team. So for those long, loud minutes, the people in the town (and the actor closing the show with a soliloquy the audience could barely hear) were subjected to the alarm bells of fire late at night, all because the basketball team had won the semi-finals and would be competing in the state championship. This same school didn't blare sirens to alert the town when a student club won an academic competition, or when a collaborative group contributed a solution to a problem that helped the community. I'm not suggesting that we should have fire sirens for every accomplishment or good deed. Rather, I am suggesting that our love of team sports might be tempered with a passion for the health and fitness of *all* our children, serving them well into adulthood. Team sports have their place, but physical education ought to be offered thoughtfully, meaningfully, and most every day to all children.

It's important to bring children outside as well. Students spend an inordinate amount of time indoors, which diminishes opportunities to both move their bodies and experience wonder and reverence in nature. Lack of time outdoors may also lead to biophobia, an aversion to and fear of nature that may produce apathetic responses to environmental problems and weaken efforts to protect the ecosystems on which we all rely.

Outdoor opportunities can be selected based on region and access. Teachers can survey their surroundings and find ways to bring children outside on a regular basis, working with whatever is available. Whether a lawn, copse, or nearby park, there are many activities that can be done just as well outside as in, and unless there are serious safety issues in the school environs, children would benefit by being outside during part of every day. Is there a tree anywhere near the school? Children can sit under it while learning about the importance of pollinator species; noticing the birds and other animals that visit and make their home in the tree; observing the changes through the seasons; examining the mycelium in the soil that works in symbiosis with the tree roots; and exploring the habitat the tree provides. Choosing an outdoor setting helps botany and mycology to come alive; ecology to make greater sense; and ethology to become possible. Let's consider the outdoors as a destination for field trips as well. Is it possible to visit a pond or park or take an urban walk with the intent to notice and document urban wildlife? Rock doves (pigeons), sparrows, and squirrels make their homes even in our biggest cities, and it is fascinating to observe animals and learn about their lives. Such activities cultivate attention, observation skills, appreciation for nature and animals, joy, and adventure.

Let's individualize the curriculum for each child.

There are some school models, such as Montessori, project-based, problem-based, experiential, and democratic, that regularly include individualized curricula. Imagining differentiated curricula within the entire public-school system might seem overwhelming. With 30-plus children to teach in each class, standards to meet, and high-stakes tests to make sure students pass, how can teachers and schools be expected to personalize curricula?

Yet today's world offers opportunities to do just this. Students can use online educational programs and resources (which often track student progress, making the process of differentiation much easier for teachers), meet with mentors, participate in internships, and more. Today's generation of digital natives[31] has the capacity to learn in ways unimagined prior to the 21st century.[32] Through

---

31 The term "digital natives" was coined by Marc Prensky in his book of the same title, to describe children who have grown up with digital technology. Read his newest thinking on education at his website: http://marcprenskyarchive.com/writings.

32 TED prize winner, Sugata Mitra's TED talk "Build a School in the Cloud" offers a glimpse into the power of today's technologies to enable powerful learning even in places where otherwise disadvantaged children live without opportunities to attend school.

blended learning with online technologies and project-based/problem-based/solutionary experiences that allow students to pursue real-world accomplishments, schools can provide students with options that take advantage of today's diverse opportunities.[33] In addition to new technologies and online platforms for acquiring important reading and math skills, through MOOCs (massive open online courses) older students can choose from hundreds of courses offered by some of the greatest professors in the world, all free of charge.

We can allow students—in developmentally appropriate ways—to avail themselves of these many opportunities and incorporate what they learn into individualized plans that enable them to pursue their interests while still obtaining necessary knowledge and skills determined by both schools and society. If some children are having a hard time acquiring certain math skills, for example, the more mathematically advanced children can forge ahead to the next level. They can use an online program, coupled with mentoring oversight, while those needing more support can master the skills at their own pace.

We no longer need to decide between Spanish, French, Mandarin, or other language offerings; students and their families can choose among many world languages. Online language programs offer exciting opportunities for language acquisition, and these can be augmented by small-group work with a fluent teacher who can help students practice conversing, as well as provide lessons about the cultures

---

33 The book *Moonshots in Education* by Esther Wojcicki and Lance Izumi offers many resources and ideas for doing this.

where the language is spoken. For students in a region where no fluent teacher is available, free videoconferencing technologies now provide opportunities to engage teachers in other regions, which was impossible in previous generations.

Because solutionaries come with different passions and talents, an individualized curriculum is important. If a high school student finds herself interested in architecture or construction, she might pursue an internship with a green building firm, while another student interested in the hospitality industry interns with an ecotourism company, and a budding civil engineer works with a mentor in the design of sustainable cities. We regularly hear about the need to ensure that high school graduates are "college- and career-ready." I can think of few better ways to achieve this goal than to offer students opportunities for personalizing their education so that they acquire knowledge and skills relevant to the working world, while bringing a solutionary mindset that not only increases their value to an employer or college but also contributes to healthier and more just and sustainable societal systems.

We could go even further by developing and offering high school Solutionary Career Certification (SCC) tracks so that students who participate in internships and mentorships in solutionary-focused professions can obtain an SCC that demonstrates to future employers and colleges a high level of real-world preparedness.[34] The goal isn't to encourage students to choose a lifelong career when they are still teenagers; rather, the purpose is to provide students

---

34 You can find more about Solutionary Career Certifications, an
     extension of CTE, in the Appendix.

with opportunities to explore and test out their interests and to develop them meaningfully.

To make school as relevant and meaningful as possible to young people who are on the verge of major personal decision-making, and to help them direct their learning toward their own goals, concerns, and dreams, imagine if teachers invited students to ask themselves and seek answers to the following four questions:

1. What challenges in my community and the world most concern me?
2. What do I love to do?
3. What am I good at?
4. What do I need to learn?

When people discover the place where the answers to the first three questions meet, and then seek out the answer to the fourth, they have opened the door to perhaps the greatest possibility for achieving a life of great purpose, meaning, and joy.

While young people don't yet know all the things they are, or will be, good at (adults don't know this fully, either), they can be encouraged to identify a range of skills and talents beyond the subject categories that they've been graded on in school. Such introspection may help them discover that they're good at mediating conflicts, listening, observing, building coalitions, organizing, collaborating, being persuasive, fact-checking and investigating, being equanimous in tense situations, being efficient, making connections among ideas, creating art, designing, writing songs, coding, and much more. Recognizing these skills and talents will empower students whose self-esteem may have suffered because they've been judged on limited criteria that haven't revealed their unique combination of positive attributes, talents, and skills.

Imagine if schools helped adolescents embark upon this journey of discovery by inviting students' deepest questions; by helping them to explore a variety of issues, experiences, and opportunities to uncover their talents, concerns, and interests; and ultimately by enabling them to acquire the knowledge and capacities they need to achieve their goals while simultaneously making the world a better place.

Let's make school meaningful and joyful.

Most of us learn best when we understand and embrace the meaning and purpose behind what we are studying. It is enjoyable and deeply engaging to solve problems we care about, to create, learn, and think. And it is joy-inducing to be of real service to others. When I was writing my book *Most Good, Least Harm: A Simple Principle for a Better World and Meaningful Life*, I conducted a survey, asking hundreds of people what brought them joy. Although I received plenty of expected responses (being with family and loved ones, being in nature, connecting with beloved animals, etc.), I also received repeated responses that doing good in the world, helping, and serving a purpose greater than oneself brought joy.

It is not uncommon for people to say that they hate (or, if they are adults, hated) school, or that school is boring. To me, boring children in school is a travesty. To take human beings at arguably the most curious and creative time of their lives and systematically dull and sometimes crush their curiosity and creativity is not only bad for children, it's bad for our world. School simply should not be a stress-inducing, unfriendly, uninspiring place. It should not be an endurance test or a battleground. For too many children (as well as too many teachers), however, it is all these things and worse. Given that learning is inherently enjoyable, it is deeply distressing that school is ever a place that lacks meaning and joy.

Imagine if every child and adolescent awoke eager to go to school to learn, innovate, participate in the arts, be kind, persevere, and discover how to become the best and brightest person they are meant to be—for their own sake and the sake of all those whom their lives affect. Our children spend such a large percentage of their lives in school. How could we want any less for them?

If you are a teacher or school administrator, ask yourself what role you can play in making your classes and school a place where students are eager to come each day, and where learning is a joyful process with great meaning. The following questions may help guide you:

1. Do your students understand and embrace the purpose behind their studies with you? How do you know? If not, how can you remedy this?

2. Do your students have the opportunity to utilize the knowledge, skills, and capacities they are gaining for real-world impact? If not, how might you provide such opportunities?

3. Do your students have the chance to pursue accomplishments that make a difference for themselves

and others? If not, what tasks and goals might you help them pursue?

It may seem that these questions place an undue amount of responsibility on teachers, and this may seem unfair if the system in which teachers work does not provide the support, trust, time, or professional development opportunities to make the necessary changes. Yet no harm can come—and great good will certainly follow for both teachers and students—from endeavoring to ensure that school is as meaningful, inspiring, purposeful, and intellectually enriching as possible. Below I offer some thoughts about supporting teachers in this effort.

Let's invest fully in teachers so that they can become solutionary educators.

Teachers have the profound and enormous responsibility to educate, mentor, motivate, hold accountable, love, and support their students. It is teachers' responsibility to ensure that students are learning and mastering content while simultaneously assuring that they are also developing powerful thinking, communication, and collaboration abilities. It is also teachers' obligation to cultivate and foster among their students qualities such as compassion, kindness, integrity, honesty, fairness, and responsibility. And to fulfill all these expectations, teachers must model these qualities themselves. Included in this quite extraordinary job description is the necessity that teachers work from early morning until very late many nights and during part of almost every weekend, all for a modest salary.

There's more. If teachers work within the current public-school system in the U.S., they may have little autonomy as professionals. They will often be required to teach classes specifically to make sure that their students do well on largely irrelevant standardized tests. If teachers bring real-world, potentially controversial issues into classrooms for exploration and solutionary thinking by students, they may be reprimanded. They may have too many students in their classroom to possibly attend to the needs of each, and they may have students who need significant individual attention that is impossible to provide. They may regularly feel compelled to spend their own money to purchase supplies, books, and even food for the children they are charged to educate.

Given all these factors, is it any wonder that many teachers are demoralized and frustrated, and that such a large percentage of new teachers leave the profession after only a few years? It's not like this everywhere. In Finland, teaching is a coveted career. Teachers there have similar status to physicians, and gaining entry into the teaching profession is highly competitive. Finnish teachers collaborate regularly, yet are autonomous in making decisions for their classrooms and in conducting student assessments.[35] And schools across Finland—whether in rural, urban, suburban, wealthy, or working

---

35 See Center on International Education Benchmarking, "Finland: Teacher and Principal Equality," n.d., http://www.ncee. org/programs-affiliates/center-on-international-education-benchmarking/top-performing-countries/finland-overview/ finland-teacher-and-principal-quality.

class communities—are equally successful at educating students.[36] In Japan,[37] teachers are paid significantly more than in the U.S., yet the country spends much less on education in general. Japanese teachers are expected not only to ensure that their students have learned the core disciplines and skills, but also to have built character and be model citizens. Teachers receive support, mentorship, and plenty of time for interaction and collaboration.

It is essential that we invest in and support the education profession, thereby attracting and welcoming bright, creative people to bring their knowledge and skills to classrooms where they will be coached and mentored by our finest teachers until they are masterful educators themselves. And it is vital that we treat the teaching profession with the respect it deserves and give teachers the autonomy to make decisions for their classrooms and students; the space and time for collaboration with fellow educators; frequent, high-quality professional development; and equitable compensation. Without achieving all these factors, it is unrealistic to expect to attract and retain excellent teachers who will be able to successfully meet the extraordinary job description presented above.

---

36 See Maria Annala, "The Place Where Ranking Schools Proves They're Actually Equal," *The Atlantic*, November 27, 2015, http://www.theatlantic.com/education/archive/2015/11/ranking-high-schools-in-finland/417333.

37 Watch Celia Hatton, "Respect for Japanese Teachers Means Top Results," CBS, September 29, 2010, on Japanese teaching, http://www.cbsnews.com/news/respect-for-japanese-teachers-means-top-results.

When I was in college my boyfriend was a medical student. One day he told me that he thought that being a physician was the most noble profession. I remember feeling irritated by his comment, not only because I thought it was silly to rank professions based on their nobility, but also because I'd gone to college pre-med and had abandoned that path, so I was probably feeling defensive. The comment stuck with me, and decades later I found myself reflecting on it. While I still believe that ranking professions on a nobility scale is not a valuable endeavor, if pressed to do so, I would say that teaching is the most noble profession. This is because there is no other profession that holds the future in its hands. Will the future be bright? The answer lies more with teachers than any other professionals. Given this, I believe we must fully support teachers in their effort to educate a generation of solutionaries.

Let's showcase students' solutions.

If schools adopt the ideas in this book, students will be working to solve real-world problems, and it behooves us to share and showcase their good ideas. Business leaders, social entrepreneurs, and investors can help turn students' ideas into meaningful, socially helpful, and potentially lucrative products and services. Legislators can sponsor new bills suggested by students that lead to healthy, positive changes for all. Media can share students' solutions with a wider audience.

To achieve this, schools can have solutionary centers and/or solutionary weeks to share students' viable answers to problems they've tackled in their schoolwork. The auditorium or gym can become the center for solutionary performances; the walls can display solutionary visual arts; the computer room can showcase the programming, videos, and public service announcements students produce to solve challenges and educate others; and an area in the school can be set aside as a store where students sell the solutionary products and services they've designed.

Science Fairs can morph into Solutionary Fairs through which students share, display, and compete for real-world opportunities as well as awards to further implement the most promising solutions, whether they emerge from the sciences, computer technologies, social studies, communications, or the arts.

Imagine how profoundly worthwhile children's education will become when their deep thinking, dedicated effort, and innovative ideas result in solutions worthy of a public audience, monetary support, and community implementation. Imagine how fully engaged and enlivened the entire school community—students, teachers, administrators, and parents—will be. And imagine the vast numbers of enthusiastic solutionaries who will graduate well on their way to contributing to a better world.[38]

Final Thoughts

The consequences of continuing to pursue our current

---

38 At the Institute for Humane Education we are helping to showcase students' solutionary work ourselves through our curated Solutionary YouTube Channel as well as an award process to help the best solutions to be implemented. Criteria can be found through links on our website here: https://humaneeducation. org/solutionary-hub/become-a-solutionary.

educational path include more disengaged children, more demoralized teachers, and the likely escalation of grave local and global challenges because young people will graduate ill-prepared to meet and address these challenges successfully.

At the beginning of this book, I shared my belief that we can solve the challenges we face in the world. As we all know, however, we might fail to solve our problems and instead bequeath to future generations a bleak future in a less and less habitable world. Tragically, it is indeed possible that we will avoid addressing climate change effectively, or in time to reverse its worst effects, and that half of all species on Earth will become extinct by the end of this century.

It is possible that coral reefs, rainforests, and glaciers will continue to disappear, and that more and more environmental refugees will be forced to flee flooded or desertified countries.

It is possible that the unrest caused by a growing human population, coupled with inequity, suffering, and lack of access to essential but scarce resources, will increase violence and warfare.

It is possible that misinformation, disinformation, polarization, and conspiracy theories will continue to gain traction, limiting knowledge about what is actually true and diminishing motivation for solutionary thinking. Should this darker future be realized, I believe that the primary reason will be because we failed to transform how and what we teach children.

I leave you with a final thought experiment. Imagine what our world will look like if schools embrace a vision of schooling in which:

- Qualities such as compassion, kindness, integrity, perseverance, honesty, fairness, and responsibility are cultivated and modeled every day.
- Each child's interests and talents are fostered and celebrated.
- Students become excellent researchers, and critical, systems, strategic, and creative thinking and collaboration are all taught and practiced diligently.
- Real-world, viable solutions to problems provide an important and respected measure of learning, along with a true sense of meaningful accomplishment.
- Self-reflective and restorative practices[39] lead to better self-management and more positive communication, ethical choice-making, deeper empathy, and more effective collaboration.
- The arts are offered regularly and lead to greater creativity, innovation, and joy.
- Physical education is a daily practice leading to better health, fitness, and wellbeing.
- The goal of schooling is to graduate solutionaries who have learned to put their skills, knowledge, and talents in service of a more just, humane, and sustainable world through whatever careers and life choices they pursue.

---

39   See Larry Ferlazzo, "Ways to Implement Restorative Practices in the Classroom," *Education Week*, January 9, 2020, https://www.edweek.org/teaching-learning/opinion-ways-to-implement-restorative-practices-in-the-classroom/2020/01.

When I imagine a generation of solutionaries, I can see the grave problems in the world being solved. I can see our broken political systems, our inequitable economic systems, our unsustainable energy systems, our inhumane and destructive agricultural systems, our unjust and polluting production systems, our dysfunctional and discriminatory criminal justice systems, our costly healthcare systems, and so many other systems made more equitable, sustainable, and compassionate. Further, I can see vibrant, joyful young people not only well prepared and positioned for the challenges they face in the present, but ready for whatever emerges in the future.

To be successful at changing our educational system and overcoming resistance, we can:

- Empower and support teachers as they transition to becoming the transformational, solutionary leaders in society they are meant to be.
- Develop and provide respectful, useful, and appropriate professional development for teachers and administrators and venues for sharing experiences to collaboratively and creatively learn from one another.[40]
- Launch a movement to transform all schools into solutionary schools that are designed around pedagogy, curricula, and practices that foster real-

---

40 The Institute for Humane Education offers online graduate programs, a Solutionary Micro-credential program, workshops, and free downloadable solutionary guidebooks, lesson plans, and curricula. Find out more at www.HumaneEducation.org.

world accomplishments, interdisciplinary subject matter, differentiated learning, and solutionary thinking and action.[41]

- Demonstrate and document that students are capable of far more than the current system expects, and that children succeed best in highly experiential, cooperative, creative, compassionate, equitable, purposeful learning environments.

- Engage all constituencies in this endeavor—not just teachers, school administrators, parents, and students. Schools exist in widely divergent communities and yet are often isolated from those communities. How children are educated will have lasting effects on the future of all life on Earth, and therefore we are all stakeholders. Let's all participate in the system of schooling and transform it into a solutionary system by paying attention to what happens in the field of education; speaking out; contacting our elected officials and electing those legislators and school board members who will work for meaningful shifts in education; drafting and sharing policy ideas; writing op-ed pieces, letters to the editor, blogs, and articles; offering and/or attending presentations; and showing up for change.

The United States and many other countries mandate a free, appropriate, and accessible education for every child. This mandate is a great privilege and responsibility. Let's not squander this opportunity. Rather, let's embrace it with

---

41 In the Appendix you'll find more suggestions for such a model.

vigor and commitment so that we truly educate young people in ways that are most meaningful and relevant to their lives and futures.

For the sake of our children and our world, please become involved in this critical endeavor. After all, the world becomes what we teach.

APPENDIX

In this Appendix, you'll find examples of where and how the ideas in this book are taking root, a 14-step solutionary process, and a vision and suggestions for transforming all schools into solutionary schools. My hope is that you will use, share, and implement what follows.

As described earlier, The Institute for Humane Education (IHE) has produced a free digital *Solutionary Guidebook* for teachers and a companion free digital guide for students and change-makers, *How to Be a Solutionary*. Both of these have been translated into many languages. We encourage students to share their solutionary efforts and ideas with us via video for potential inclusion on our Solutionary YouTube Channel. We are also providing awards to students who produce the most solutionary solutions. Additionally, we offer free lesson plans, issues guides, and curricula in the Teacher Resources section of the Solutionary Hub on our website as well as a Solutionary Micro-credential Program for teachers, and online graduate programs with Antioch University (M.Ed., M.A., Ed.D., and Graduate Certificate).

As you utilize and implement these materials and ideas, please share your experiences, successes, and challenges with us. We hope to learn from you and improve education together.

Thanks for all you do,

Zoe

zoe@HumaneEducation.org

www.HumaneEducation.org

WHERE SOLUTIONARY LEARNING IS TAKING ROOT

The first edition of this book, published in 2016, sparked solutionary learning in a number of places, and I'm highlighting three examples to demonstrate how these ideas can take root in:

- An entire county
- A school district
- A classroom

SAN MATEO COUNTY, CA

After reading this book, Andra Yeghoian, the Environmental Literacy Coordinator at the Office of Education in San Mateo County, CA, shared it with the curriculum and instructional development team for the county, which serves approximately 113,000 students in twenty-three school districts. The team read the book and adopted its solutionary approach as the philosophy and framework for the county. They began using these ideas in their professional development workshops, fellowship programs, and summer institutes offered to hundreds of teachers.

In turn, teachers throughout the county produced Solutionary Units for their classrooms. The STEM team in the Office of Education then planned the first annual Solutionary Fair. One hundred and thirteen student solutionary teams registered to share their work in just the first year. San Mateo has continued its solutionary professional development institutes for teachers and produced a number of resources that educators anywhere can use to operationalize the ideas in this book.[1] I am hopeful that San Mateo will represent the first of many counties to adopt a solutionary framework for education and hold solutionary fairs to showcase student solutions.

OCEANSIDE SCHOOL DISTRICT, NY

Mitch Bickman, the Director of Social Studies for the Oceanside School District on Long Island, NY, is integrating solutionary learning into the entire K–12 social studies curriculum for the district.

Thus far, the high school has offered an annual multidisciplinary solutionary unit, which revolves around the Sustainable Development Goals (SDGs), to 10th and 11th graders through the History and English departments. The students identify issues related to the SDGs that they are passionate about, focus on a specific topic, and use the solutionary process described in the *Solutionary Guidebook* to provide the framework for students to devise and implement solutions.

In March 2020, the high school students who completed solutionary units led and mentored the district's 5th graders at the district's first "World We Want" Solutionary Fair. During the fair, the high schoolers introduced the 5th

---

1   You can find San Mateo's framework here: https://docs.google.com/document/d/1cbqGYDvUJmN5uZKaHmj0SkYwvaH749SDJnPfvs8wcus/edit#.

graders to the SDGs and created stations to educate and excite them about different solutionary concepts, all in preparation for their ongoing solutionary learning in middle school.

I attended Oceanside's first Solutionary Fair and was deeply moved by the incredible enthusiasm of the high school mentors, the excitement of the fifth graders, and the dedication of the teachers and administrators. With several schools participating, there is great potential for district-wide contributions, cross-pollination of ideas at events like the fair described above, and a community solutionary mindset taking hold as solutionary learning becomes infused into the entire K–12 social studies curriculum.

EVERGREEN MIDDLE SCHOOL, CO

Julia Fliss is a 6th-grade language arts teacher at Evergreen Middle School in Evergreen, CO. She'd been teaching her students about the Sustainable Development Goals (SDGs), and after downloading the *Solutionary Guidebook* in 2020, as well as reading the first edition of this book, she began using the solutionary process to "activate and develop a solutionary mindset" among her students in order to enable them to design, launch, and carry out their SDG-based Personalized Action Projects.

Julia invites her students to identify problems and concerns in their community and then helps them cultivate solutionary thinking to discover how they can best make a difference. Using root cause diagrams, her students examine the complexity of and interconnections between the problems they identify, along with the systems that perpetuate them, and then develop solutions that do the most good and the least harm.

Integrating information and media literacy lessons, Julia has her students research, synthesize, collaborate, and co-create "InfoMurals" to share their learning with each other and practice persuasive speaking. Next, her students take action. They choose their scope, goals, and platform and make a measurable positive impact in their community. In 2021 Julia initiated the first Solutionary Summit to enable students to share their work.

Julia's approach to teaching and learning—in which she makes her classroom real-world and solutionary-focused—is exactly the goal of this book. By helping her students to bring a solutionary lens to all issues and problems, Julia is leading the way for the emergence of a solutionary generation.

THE SOLUTIONARY PROCESS

At the Institute for Humane Education we have create a 14-step Solutionary Process that is described in detail in both the free digital *Solutionary Guidebook* for educators and the free *How to Be a Solutionary* guide for students and change-makers. Here you'll find a condensed version to help you get started teaching your students to be solutionaries. It's worthwhile to go through this process yourself, choosing a problem of concern to you, so that you have some experience before guiding your students.

1. Cultivate compassion.
Introduce your students to issues in their community and the world that impact people, animals, and the environment. Share stories of individuals (people and animals) who are experiencing challenges or enduring suffering to awaken and foster their compassion.

2. Learn about issues in your community and in the world.
Invite your students to learn more about the issues you brought to their attention in step 1, encouraging them to focus on an issue that they care about deeply. Have them conduct research and investigate the issue to gain a solid understanding of it.

3. Identify a specific problem you care about solving.

Have your students identify a specific problem that they uncover in their research—one they want to solve. Have them write a clear problem statement to guide their solutionary work.

4. Connect with stakeholders and those working to solve the problem.

Help your students connect with everyone they can who has a stake in the problem, including those who are already working to solve it. Stakeholders include not only those who are harmed by the problem (or the people representing them if the problem revolves around animals or the environment), but also those who are benefiting from the problem and the systems that support it.

5. Identify the causes of the problem from systemic structures to psychological factors, worldviews, and mindsets.

Using a systems thinking methodology like the one described in the *Solutionary Guidebook*, have students dive deeper into their research and investigation to understand the societal systems that are causing and perpetuating the problem, as well as the deeper causes—such as beliefs, mindsets, and psychological factors—that have led us to create those systems.

6. Determine who and what is harmed by the problem, and who and what benefits.

Problems usually impact more than we initially notice. Have

students identify *everyone* who is impacted, both positively and negatively, including all people, animals, and the environment.

7. Research what has been done to solve the problem thus far.

Have your students investigate the different solutions that have already been tried. What's worked? What's failed? What great ideas could be improved upon? What systems are preventing good solutions from spreading widely and becoming fully implemented?

8. Devise solutions that address the causes of the problem, and which do the most good and least harm to people, animals, and the environment.

Mentor and support your students as they develop solutions that address the *causes* of the problem, so it doesn't continue. Help them understand that humanitarian and charitable acts, while important, won't prevent the problem from persisting. Guide them in devising solutions that do the most good and least harm to everyone, so that their solutions don't cause unintended negative consequences to any groups or individuals, whether human or nonhuman.

9. Determine which solutions are most solutionary and most feasible for implementation.

Assist your students as they identify which of their ideas are (a) most solutionary and (b) most practical for implementation. Use the Solutionary Scale to help them identify (a).

EMERGING	DEVELOPING	SOLUTIONARY	MOST SOLUTIONARY
The solution, while well-intentioned, does not yet address rood and/or systemic causes (and may produce unintended negative consequences to people, animals, or the environment).	The solution addresses root and/or systemic causes but produces unintended negative consequences to people, animals, or the environment.	The solution addresses root and/or systemic causes and strives not to produce unintended negative consequences to people, animals, or the environment.	The solution **significantly and strategically** addresses root and/or systemic causes and does not harm people, animals, or the environment.

The most feasible solution will be the one they are both excited about implementing *and* have the capacity to put into effect. NOTE: the most solutionary solution may not be the most feasible, so help your students find the sweet spot where they have the means to put one of their solutionary ideas into practice. It's possible that they'll come up with a solutionary way to put an existing, but languishing, solution into effect. This is a great way to be a solutionary!

10. Create a plan to implement your solution.

Using this planning chart as a guide (described in more detail in the *Solutionary Guidebook*), support your students in completing their plan.

Action Steps (Be specific)	Individuals Involved (Including stakeholders)	Resources Needed	Timeline (Date by which the action should be completed)	Potential Difficulties	What does success look like and how will we evaluate it?

11. Implement your solution.

Support your students in implementing their solutions to the greatest degree possible within the constraints of your classroom and curriculum.

12. Present your work.

Ideally, your students will present their work in a classroom, school, and/or district forum, such as a Solutionary Fair or Solutionary Summit. We encourage students to follow the guidelines described in our guidebooks—or create their own innovative approach—for video submissions to the Institute for Humane Education for potential inclusion in our curated Solutionary YouTube Channel as well as to be eligible for an award.

13. Assess, share, iterate.

We all become better solutionaries when we carefully evaluate our solutions, inform others by sharing our successes (as well as our failures), and make improvements along the way. Help your students to self-reflect, collect meaningful feedback and data, and adjust their solutionary efforts.

14. Celebrate!

Don't forget to celebrate your students' good work. Here are some ideas:

- Host a mural-making party during which students share images and words to depict the world solutionaries like them will create.

- Hold a Solutionary Council in which students publicly state why each classmate in the circle is a solutionary.

- Plan a "good news" class highlighting the positive actions and outcomes of young solutionaries in the classroom and beyond.

WHAT IF ALL SCHOOLS BECAME SOLUTIONARY SCHOOLS?

Let's think big. Let's imagine that all schools become solutionary schools. What would the foundational philosophy, purpose, and approaches look like? Below are some ideas developed by a team at the Institute for Humane Education to help get us started.

A Purpose, Vision, Mission, and Promise Statement for Solutionary Schools

Purpose of Solutionary Schools
- To provide young people with an engaging, personalized, real world–oriented education that serves their full development as human beings in an interdependent world.
- To provide the world with motivated, knowledgeable, and compassionate citizens who have demonstrable abilities to solve real-world problems successfully, collaboratively, creatively, and wisely.

Vision for Solutionary School Communities
Kind, creative, skilled, knowledgeable, and joyful people learning together and co-creating a thriving world for all people, animals, and the ecosystems that sustain life.

Mission of Solutionary Schools

To educate students to be solutionaries who are:

- Loved, supported, and appreciated for their unique qualities, interests, and talents.
- Helped to become compassionate and responsible people with integrity.
- Provided with opportunities to gain knowledge and skills in order to become excellent critical, systems, strategic, scientific, logical, and creative thinkers and collaborators who are able to pursue goals that are personally meaningful, and which contribute to a more just, humane, and sustainable world.

Promise of Solutionary Schools

To provide young people with an education that cultivates and honors all their capacities as human beings, solutionary schools will:

- Ensure that students acquire excellent research and thinking capacities (students demonstrate highly developed critical, systems, strategic, creative, scientific, analytic, design, mathematical, and logical thinking).
- Foster emotional health and excellent communication (students demonstrate compassion, kindness, self-awareness, motivation for good, fairness, honesty, active listening, and effective, respectful writing, speaking, and videography).

- Provide opportunities for genuine accomplishments in which students solve real-world problems, demonstrate collaboration, engage in the community, and are able to pursue solutionary-focused internships and opportunities.
- Offer daily opportunities for creativity through the expressive arts as well as physical exercise and practice.

Foundational Understandings of Solutionary Schools

1. **A humane, just, and healthy world is possible.**
   So many things have improved dramatically, which reminds us that a better future attainable. We can and must learn how to live wisely and peacefully; to create equitable, humane, and sustainable systems; and to protect the biosphere on which all life depends.

2. **We are inextricably connected, ecologically and societally.**
   What we each do and do not do affects people, animals, and the environment. Ecological and social systems interact, and we have the capacity to discover these interactions and interconnections and act compassionately and with integrity.

3. **We are all responsible.**
   To the degree that we are able, we each have a responsibility to contribute to the creation of healthy, equitable, peaceful, and humane systems and to solve the challenges we face, as well as to strive to make

ethical choices that do the most good and least harm for all people, especially the most marginalized; for all animals; and for the ecosystems that sustain life.

4. **Solutions are dependent upon accurate information and multiple perspectives.**

   We can and must learn to identify credible information; to distinguish fact from conjecture and misinformation/disinformation; to reason; and to seek out a variety of perspectives to inform our opinions and efforts.

5. **Solutionary solutions emerge from solutionary thinking.**

   Either/or thinking limits our capacity to identify and create innovative, visionary solutions that work for all. We can and must strive to develop solutions that move beyond simplistic, dichotomous responses in order to discover the most successful and comprehensive answers to problems.

6. **An ideal solution does not harm people, animals, or the ecosystems that sustain life.**

   We can and must strive to find solutions that are sustainable, just, and humane toward all beings and the environment and that respect both individual humans and nonhumans and the commons we share.

7. **An ideal solution addresses root and/or systemic causes.**

   While treating symptoms of problems is often important, to solve systemic challenges we can and must identify and address the underlying root and/or systemic causes that lead to problems.

Important Elements of Solutionary Schools

- **Solutionary-focused Curriculum**: The curriculum is real-world and solutionary-focused, relevant to both students' lives and the world, personalized, modifiable, and updated regularly.
- **Solutionary Centers**: Solutionary Centers within the school showcase student solutions through any/all of the following: examples of implemented ideas, solutionary theater and the arts, solutionary presentations and summits (live-streamed to the world during day-long events), maker spaces, exhibition areas, entrepreneurial opportunities through a solutionary store that sells students' solutionary products and services, and more.
- **Student Support**: Students are loved, nurtured, and supported to discover and develop their unique gifts and their capacities to best contribute. Restorative practices have replaced punitive disciplinary policies.
- **Solutionary Career Certificates (SCCs)**: Students are able to pursue a certificate(s) in a solutionary field(s) of their choice.
- **Emphasis on the Whole Child**: The school provides a balance between academic subjects, the arts and design, and physical, mental, and emotional wellness to ensure that students are able to cultivate and utilize their thinking, affective, creative, and physical capacities synergistically and positively for the benefit of themselves and others.
- **Assessment**: Assessments are constructed to best help children learn, accomplish, and develop their research

skills, thinking capacities, collaborative abilities, solutionary ideas, and knowledge, and to achieve their personal goals and the goals of the school.

- **Democracy:** To the degree possible, all school members (students, faculty, administration, parents, staff) have a voice in school decision-making.
- **Faculty:** All teachers are expected to continually strive for excellence and to embrace being a worthy role model for children. They receive competitive compensation, are respected as professionals, receive professional development and training in solutionary-focused humane education, and contribute to the continual refinement of the curriculum.
- **Most Good, Least Harm Ethic:** To the degree possible, the school models choices that do the most good and least harm for people, animals, and the environment, taking into account those who are most marginalized. In practice, these choices may include (but are not limited to): renewable energy; sustainable building materials/furniture; active attention to product usage and recycling; fair trade policies for school purchases; a cafeteria that chooses healthy, humanely, justly, and sustainably produced food; school garden/living walls that contribute to the cafeteria and demonstrate healthy and sustainable food systems, restorative practices, etc.
- **Values:** The following qualities are actively cultivated among the entire school community (students, faculty, administrators, staff): compassion, responsibility, kindness, honesty, fairness, integrity, perseverance, self-awareness, positive communication and active listening, wonder and curiosity, creativity, and collaboration.

- **Inclusive and Systemic Solutionary Approach**: The school eschews either/or thinking and always seeks solutions that are healthy, humane, and just for all.

Core Values of Solutionary Schools

The following core values and qualities are cultivated daily among all members of the school community.

Compassion

The ability to understand and relate to others and their experiences coupled with the desire to be helpful and of service.

Responsibility

The understanding that everything we do and do not do has an impact, and therefore we should do our best to make choices that do the most good and least harm for ourselves and others, including other species and the environment, and to enthusiastically participate in efforts to make systems in our society sustainable, equitable, and humane.

Kindness

The act of doing good and helping in both our interpersonal relationships and through choices that affect others who may be far-removed but with whom we are connected through globalized systems.

Perseverance

The effort to pursue goals even in the face of obstacles and setbacks.

Self-Awareness

The ability to observe and understand ourselves, our impact on others, and our capacities, talents, passions, and struggles. Engagement in introspection and reflection.

Positive Communication and Active Listening

The commitment to pay attention to others, welcome divergent voices, understand the power of language, and consider differing perspectives and experiences.

Wonder and Curiosity

The ability to marvel and experience awe and amazement, coupled with the desire to know and understand.

Creativity

The practice of innovation, making things, designing, improvising, putting ideas together that didn't exist before, and developing new thoughts and perspectives that matter.

Collaboration

The effort to learn from and with one another and work together toward common goals.

Honesty

The quality of being truthful, straightforward, and sincere.

Fairness

The commitment to equity and justice such that everyone receives what they need to survive and thrive, including access to opportunity, resources, and support.

Integrity

The commitment to live according to all these values to the best of our ability and do what is consistent with the above when no one is looking.

Solutionary Dispositions, Abilities, Literacies, and Competencies

Dispositions

- Committed to choice-making that does the most good and least harm for oneself and others, including other species
- Compassionate
- Conscientious
- Ethical
- Mindful
- Open-minded
- Solutions-oriented

Thinking Abilities

- Ability to conduct research and analyze for validity
- Ability to consider different viewpoints, experiences, and perspectives
- Ability to make causal interconnections
- Ability to transfer knowledge
- Design thinking
- Logical thinking
- Mathematical thinking
- Scientific thinking
- Solutionary thinking, comprised primarily of:
    - Critical thinking
    - Systems thinking
    - Strategic thinking
    - Creative thinking

Literacies and Competencies

- Collaborative competency
- Computer/technology competency
- Financial/economic literacy
- Foundational verbal and written literacy
- Foundational numeracy
- Foundational scientific literacy
- Global awareness literacy
- Media literacy (including literacy around disinformation and misinformation)
- Problem finding competency
- Problem solving competency
- Project management competency
- Root and systemic cause analysis
- Structural oppression literacy

Communication and Expression Skills

- Ability to advocate effectively
- Active listening skills
- Artistic skills
- Conflict resolution skills
- Cross-cultural communication skills
- Public speaking skills
- Writing skills
- Videography skills

Solutionary Career Certification Tracks

In some schools, students are able to pursue a CTE (Career and Technical Education) in fields such as plumbing, construction, landscaping, and electrical work. These certification tracks allow students to gain important life experiences and skills that prepare them for employment upon high school graduation. This approach to employment opportunity and job security can be expanded to embrace solutionary career tracks as well.

There are many possibilities for Solutionary Career Certification (SCC) tracks that students can pursue in high school. Any career, job, or profession can be solutionary; what matters is that practitioners understand and embrace their responsibility to ensure that the systems within that profession or job are ethical, sustainable, and healthy for people, animals, and the environment. Some fields are more obviously solutionary than others. In the list below, you'll find professions and jobs that are, by their nature, generally solutionary, as well as other fields explicitly modified to have a solutionary focus.

This list represents a small portion (with some personal additions) of those identified by school developer, school director, and Institute for Humane Education M.Ed. graduate, Marion MacGillivray. Students participating in an SCC can pursue and receive certification for a certain number of hours of study, internships, mentoring, and accomplishments. Students may be able to gain substantial proficiency in some of these tracks, while in others their certification will specify a more narrow focus and specific accomplishment geared toward professional preparation.

Agriculture: sustainable farming; permaculture; soil regeneration; restorative forestry; myco-remediation; plant-based protein development; cultivated meat development; organic gardening and landscaping; renewable-energy hydroponics

Architecture, Design, Construction, Building Trades: green architecture; sustainable design; restorative land-use planning; eco-friendly building and furniture production; energy efficiency; solar and wind design and installation; sustainable trade specialties (carpentry, electrical, plumbing, insulation, painting, flooring, etc.)

Art and Theater: solutionary-focused: playwriting; filmmaking; performance poetry; puppetry; dance; improvisational and/or stand up comedy; story-telling; media entertainment; visual arts (photography, sculpture, fine art)

Communication: investigative reporting; documentary production; solutionary-focused writing, illustration, graphic design, and publishing; campaigning; public speaking; advocacy

Business, Management, and Administration: social business development; nonprofit start-ups and management; green consulting; ethical investing; fundraising and grant writing; public service advertising; microfinance

Education and Training: humane education; teaching; solutionary curriculum development; solutionary workshop facilitation

Government and Public Administration: policy-making; political action and service; legislative aid work; solutionary think tanks

Health and Medicine: preventive health care; nutritional science and consulting; counseling and social work; fitness; solutionary-focused medicine

Hospitality and Tourism: volunteer tourism; ecotourism; educational tourism; solutionary tourism

Law, Public Safety, Corrections, Security: environmental, social justice, and animal protection law; restorative justice; conflict resolution and peacemaking; immigration solutions

Manufacturing: fair-trade, eco-friendly, cruelty-free production; cradle to cradle production;[2] recycling

STEM (Science, Technology, Engineering, Math) Careers: green chemistry; humane research; civil engineering for sustainable cities and towns; non-polluting/regenerative transportation systems; clean energy systems

---

2   Cradle to cradle refers to production that isn't simply *less* toxic or destructive, but which is actually nourishing and helpful to the environment. The book *Cradle to Cradle* by William McDonough and Michael Braungart details such a vision for production.

FURTHER READING AND RESOURCES

Books Primarily on Education

Berger, Warren. *A More Beautiful Question: The Power of Inquiry to Spark Breakthrough Ideas.* New York: Bloomsbury USA, 2014.

Berry, Barnett, et al. *Teaching 2030: What We Must Do for Our Students and Our Public Schools . . . Now and in the Future.* New York: Teachers College Press, 2011.

Block, Joshua. *Teaching for a Living Democracy: Project-Based Learning for the English and History Classroom.* New York: Teachers College Press, 2020.

Burger, Edward B., and Michael Starbird. *The 5 Elements of Effective Thinking.* Princeton, NJ: Princeton University Press, 2012.

Chaltain, Sam. *Our School: Searching for Community in the Era of Choice.* New York: Teachers College Press, 2014.

Chapin, Dexter. *Master Teachers: Making a Difference on the Edge of Chaos.* Lanham, MD: Rowman & Littlefield Education, 2008.

Christensen, Linda, and Stan Karp, Eds. *Rethinking School Reform: Views from the Classroom.* Milwaukee, WI.: Rethinking Schools, 2003.

Cowhey, Mary. *Black Ants and Buddhists.* Portland, ME: Stenhouse Publishers, 2006.

Dintersmith, Ted. *What Schools Could Be.* Princeton, NJ: Princeton University Press, 2018.

Esquith, Rafe. *Teach Like Your Hair's on Fire*. New York: Viking, 2007.

Freire, Paulo. *Pedagogy of the Oppressed*. New York: Continuum, 2000.

Friedman, Audrey A., and Luke Reynolds, Eds. *Burned In: Fueling the Fire to Teach*. New York: Teachers College Press, 2011.

Gardner, Howard. *Five Minds for the Future*. Cambridge, MA: Harvard Business Review Press, 2009.

Gatto, John Taylor. *Dumbing Us Down: The Hidden Curriculum of Compulsory Schooling*. Gabriola Island, BC: New Society Publishers, 2002.

Goldstein, Dana. *The Teacher Wars: A History of America's Most Embattled Profession*. New York: Anchor Books, 2015.

Goleman, Daniel, Lisa Bennett, and Zenobia Barlow. *Ecoliterate: How Educators are Cultivating Emotional, Social, and Ecological Intelligence*. San Francisco: Jossey-Bass, 2012.

Gorski, Paul C. *Reaching and Teaching Students in Poverty: Strategies for Erasing the Opportunity Gap*. New York: Routledge, 2017

Goyal, Nikhil. *Schools on Trial: How Freedom and Creativity Can Fix Our Educational Malpractice*. New York: Doubleday, 2016.

Hunter, John. *World Peace and Other 4th-Grade Achievements*. New York: Houghton Mifflin, 2013.

Jacobs, Heidi Hayes. *Curriculum 21: Essential Education for a Changing World*. Alexandria, VA: ASCD, 2010.

Johnson, LouAnne. *The Queen of Education*. San Francisco: Jossey-Bass, 2007.

Khan, Salman. *The One World Schoolhouse: Education Reimagined*. New York: Twelve, 2012.

Kohn, Alfie. *Schooling Beyond Measure and Other Unorthodox Essays About Education*. Portsmouth, NH: Heinemann, 2015.

Kottler, Jeffrey A., Stanley J. Zehm, and Ellen Kottler. *On Being a Teacher: The Human Dimension, Third Edition*. Thousand Oaks, CA.: Corwin Press, 2005.

Lickona, Thomas. *Educating for Character*. New York: Bantam, 1992.

McCarthy, Colman. *I'd Rather Teach Peace*. Maryknoll, NY: Orbis Books, 2008.

McCarty, Marietta. *Little Big Minds*. New York: Penguin Group, 2006.

Meier, Deborah. *In Schools We Trust: Creating Communities of Learning in an Era of Testing and Standardization*. Boston: Beacon Press, 2014.

Merrow, John. *The Influence of Teachers: Reflections on Teaching and Leadership*. New York: LM Books, 2011.

Mintz, Jerry, and Carlo Ricci, Eds. *Turning Points: 27 Visionaries in Education Tell Their Own Stories*. Roslyn Heights, NY: Alternative Education Resource Organization, 2010.

Olson, Kirsten. *Wounded by School*. New York: Teachers College Press, 2009.

Palmer, Parker. *The Courage to Teach*. San Francisco: Jossey-Bass, 2007.

Pearlman, Steven J. *America's Critical Thinking Crisis: The Failure and Promise of Education*. PublishDrive, 2020.

Perkins, David. *Future Wise: Educating Our Children for a Changing World*. San Francisco: Jossey-Bass, 2014.

Prensky, Marc. *Education to Better Their World: Unleashing the Power of 21st Century Kids*. New York: Teachers College Press, 2016.

Reigeluth, Charles M., and Jennifer R. Karnopp. *Reinventing Schools: It's Time to Break the Mold*. Lanham, MD: Rowman & Littlefield Education, 2013.

Reynolds, Luke, Ed. *Imagine It Better: Visions of What School Might Be*. Portsmouth, NH: Heinemann, 2014.

Roberts, Rohan. *Cosmic Citizens and Moonshot Thinking: Education in an Age of Exponential Technologies*. Bloomington, IN: AuthorHouse, 2018.

Robinson, Sir Ken, and Lou Aronica. *Creative Schools: The Grassroots Revolution That's Transforming Education*. New York: Viking, 2015.

Russakoff, Dale. *The Prize: Who's in Charge of America's Schools*. New York: Houghton Mifflin Harcourt, 2015.

Schauffler, Marina. *Kids As Planners: A Guide to Strengthening Students, Schools and Communities Through Service-Learning* (Revised and Expanded 3rd Edition). Lewiston, ME: Kids Consortium, 2011.

Stern, Julie H., et al. *Learning That Transfers: Designing Curriculum for a Changing World*. Thousand Oaks, CA: Corwin, 2021.

Swope, Kathy, and Barbara Miner, Eds. *Failing Our Kids: Why the Testing Craze Won't Fix Our Schools*. Milwaukee, WI: Rethinking Schools, 2000.

Trilling, Bernie and Fadel, Charles. *21st Century Skills: Learning for Life in Our Times*. San Francisco: Jossey-Bass, 2009.

Weil, Zoe. *Above All, Be Kind: Raising a Humane Child in Challenging Times*. Gabriola Island, BC: New Society Publishers, 2003.

Wiggins, Grant, and Jay McTighe. *Understanding by Design* (Expanded 2nd Edition). Alexandria, VA: ASCD, 2005.

Wojcicki, Esther, and Lance Izumi. *Moonshots in Education:*

Launching Blended Learning in the Classroom. San Francisco: Pacific Research Institute, 2015.

Books Primarily on Human Rights and Social Justice

Alexander, Michelle. *The New Jim Crow: Mass Incarceration in the Age of Colorblindness.* New York: The New Press, 2012.

Baird, Robert M., and Stuart E. Rosenbaum, Eds. *Hatred, Bigotry, and Prejudice.* Amherst, NY: Prometheus Books, 1999.

Bales, Kevin. *Ending Slavery.* Berkeley: University of California Press, 2007.

Batstone, David. *Not for Sale: The Return of the Global Slave Trade and How We Can Fight It.* New York: HarperOne, 2010.

Cohen, Stanley. *States of Denial: Knowing About Atrocities and Suffering.* Cambridge, MA: Polity Press, 2001.

Eberhardt, Jennifer. *Biased: Uncovering the Hidden Prejudice That Shapes What We See, Think, and Do.* New York: Penguin Books, 2020.

Johnson, Allan. G. *Privilege, Power and Difference.* Boston, MA: McGraw-Hill, 2006.

Kassindja, Fauziya. *Do They Hear You When You Cry.* New York: Delta, 1999.

Kressel, Neil J. *Mass Hate: The Global Rise of Genocide and Terror.* Boulder, CO: Westview Press, 2002.

Kristof, Nicholas, and Sheryl WuDunn. *Half the Sky: Turning Oppression into Opportunity for Women Worldwide.* New York, NY: Vintage Books, 2009.

Sloan, Judith, and Warren Lehrer. *Crossing the Boulevard.* New York: W. W. Norton & Co., 2003.

Tomasevski, Katarina. *Education Denied: Costs and Remedies.* New York: Zed Books, 2003.

Wilkerson, Isabel. *Caste: The Origin of Our Discontents.* New York: Random House, 2020.

Yousafzai, Malala, and Christina Lamb. *I Am Malala: The Girl Who Stood Up for Education and Was Shot by the Taliban.* Boston, MA: Little, Brown and Company, 2013.

Yunus, Muhammad. *Creating a World Without Poverty: Social Business and the Future of Capitalism.* New York: Public Affairs, 2009.

Books Primarily on Environmental Preservation

AtKisson, Alan. *Sustainability Is for Everyone.* Oxford, UK: Isis Academy (Iffley Academy), 2013.

Berners-Lee, Michael. *How Bad Are Bananas? The Carbon Footprint of Everything.* Berkeley, CA: Greystone Books, 2011.

Diamond, Jared. *Collapse: How Societies Choose to Fail or Succeed.* New York: Penguin, 2011.

Ellis, Richard. *The Empty Ocean.* Washington, DC: Island Press, 2004.

Kolbert, Elizabeth. *The Sixth Extinction: An Unnatural History.* New York: Henry Holt & Co., 2014.

Hawken, Paul. *Drawdown: The Most Comprehensive Plan Ever Proposed to Reverse Global Warming.* New York, NY: Penguin Books, 2017.

Henley, Thom, and Kenny Peavy. *As If the Earth Matters: Recommitting to Environmental Education.* Gabriola Island, BC: New Society Publishers, 2006.

McDonough, William, and Michael Braungart. *Cradle to Cradle: Remaking the Way We Make Things*. New York: North Point Press, 2010.

Orr, David. *Earth in Mind: On Education, Environment and the Human Prospect* (2nd Edition). Washington, DC: Island Press, 2004.

Ryan, John C., and Alan Thein Durning. *Stuff: The Secret Lives of Everyday Things*. Seattle, WA: Sightline Institute, 2012.

Speth, James. *The Bridge at the End of the World*. New Haven, Conn.: Yale University Press, 2009.

Books Primarily on Animal Protection

Akhtar, Aysha. *Our Symphony with Animals: On Health, Empathy, and Our Shared Destinies*. New York: Pegasus, 2019.

Baur, Gene. *Farm Sanctuary: Changing Hearts and Minds About Animals*. New York: Touchstone, 2008.

Bekoff, Marc. *The Emotional Lives of Animals*. Novato, CA: New World Library, 2011.

Eisnitz, Gail. *Slaughterhouse*. Amherst, NY: Prometheus Books, 2007.

Foer, Jonathan Safran. *Eating Animals*. New York: Back Bay Books, 2010.

Fouts, Roger. *Next of Kin: What Chimps Taught Me About Who We Are*. New York, NY: Quill, 1997.

Ginsberg, Caryn. *Animal Impact: Proven Secrets to Achieve Results and Move the World*. Priority Ventures Group, 2011.

Joy, Melanie. *Why We Love Dogs, Eat Pigs and Wear Cows*. San Francisco, CA.: Conari Press, 2010.

Masson, Jeffrey Moussaieff. *When Elephants Weep*. New York: Delta, 1995.

McCarthur, Jo-Anne. *We Animals*. Brooklyn, NY: Lantern Books, 2013.

Patterson, Charles. *Eternal Treblinka*. Brooklyn, NY: Lantern Books, 2002.

Reitman, Judith. *Stolen for Profit*. New York: Kensington Books, 1995.

Safina, Carl. *Becoming Wild: How Animal Cultures Raise Families, Create Beauty, and Achieve Peace*: New York: Henry Holt, 2020.

Singer, Peter. *Animal Liberation*. New York, NY: Harper Perennial Modern Classics, 2009.

Stevens, Kathy. *Where the Blind Horse Sings: Love and Healing at an Animal Sanctuary*. New York: Skyhorse, 2009.

Taylor, Sunaura. *Beasts of Burden: Animal and Disability Liberation*. New York: The New Press, 2017.

Wise, Steven. *Rattling the Cage*. London: Profile, 2001.

Wulff, Gypsy. *Turning Points in Compassion: Personal Journeys of Animal Advocates*. Spirit Wings Humane Education, 2015.

Books Primarily on Culture, Progress, and Change-making

Abdullah, Sharif. *Creating a World That Works for All*. San Francisco, CA: Berrett-Koehler Publishers, 1999.

AtKisson, Alan. *Believing Cassandra: An Optimist Looks at a Pessimist's World*. London: Earthscan, 2010.

Barasch, Marc Ian. *The Compassionate Life: Walking the Path of Kindness*. San Francisco, CA: Berrett-Koehler Publishers, 2009.

Barnes, Peter. *Capitalism 3.0: A Guide to Reclaiming the Commons.* San Francisco, CA: Berrett-Koehler Publishers, 2006.

Bornstein, David. *How to Change the World.* Oxford: Oxford University Press, 2007.

Chase, Robin. *Peers Inc: How People and Platforms Are Inventing the Collaborative Economy and Reinventing Capitalism.* New York: Public Affairs, 2015.

Enriquez, Juan. *Right/Wrong: How Technology Transforms Our Ethics.* Cambridge, MA: MIT Press, 2020.

Gardner, Daniel. *The Science of Fear: How the Culture of Fear Manipulates Your Brain.* New York: Plume, 2009.

Goffman, Alice. *On the Run: Fugitive Life in an American City.* Chicago: University of Chicago Press, 2014.

Greenspan, Miriam. *Healing Through the Dark Emotions.* Boston, Mass.: Shambhala, 2004.

Haidt, Jonathan. *The Righteous Mind: Why Good People Are Divided by Politics and Religion.* New York: Vintage, 2013.

Harari, Yuval Noah. *Sapiens: A Brief History of Humankind.* New York: Harper Perennial, 2018.

Harper, A. Breeze. *Sistah Vegan: Black Women Speak on Food, Identity, Health, and Society* (10th Anniversary Edition). Brooklyn, NY: Lantern Publishing & Media, 2020.

Heath, Dan. *Upstream: The Quest to Solve Problems Before They Happen.* New York: Simon & Schuster, 2020.

Hinkley, Robert. *Time to Change Corporations: Closing the Citizenship Gap.* Scotts Valley, CA: Create Space, 2011.

Kiernan, Stephen. *Authentic Patriotism: Restoring America's Founding Ideals Through Selfless Action.* New York: St. Martin's Press, 2010.

Ko, Aph & Syl. *Aphro-ism: Essays on Pop Culture, Feminism, and Black Veganism from Two Sisters*. Brooklyn, NY: Lantern Books, 2017.

Krech, Gregg. *Naikan: Gratitude, Grace and the Art of Self Reflection*. Berkeley, CA: Stone Bridge Press, 2001.

Mckeown, Greg. *Essentialism: The Disciplined Pursuit of Less*. New York: Crown Business, 2014.

Meadows, Donnella, and Donna Wright. *Thinking in Systems: A Primer*. White River Junction, VT: Chelsea Green, 2008.

Pinker, Steven. *Enlightenment Now: The Case for Reason, Science, Humanism, and Progress*. New York: Penguin Books, 2019.

Raworth, Kate. *Doughnut Economics: Seven Ways to Think Like a 21st-Century Economist*. White River Junction, VT: Chelsea Green, 2018.

Rosling, Hans, et al. *Factfulness: Ten Reasons Why We're Wrong About the World, and Why Things Are Better Than You Think*. New York: Flatiron Books Reprint Edition, 2020

Shapiro, Paul. *Clean Meat: How Growing Meat without Animals Will Revolutionize Dinner and the World*. New York: Gallery Books, 2018.

Singer, Peter. *The Most Good You Can Do: How Effective Altruism Is Changing Ideas About Living Ethically*. New Haven, CT: Yale University Press, 2015.

Steele, Claude. *Whistling Vivaldi: How Stereotypes Affect Us and What We Can Do*. New York: Norton, 2011.

Sunstein, Cass. *Conspiracy Theories and Other Dangerous Ideas*. New York: Simon & Schuster, 2014.

Sunstein, Cass. *Wiser: Getting Beyond Groupthink to Make Groups Smarter*. Cambridge, MA: Harvard Business Review Press, 2014.

Ury, William. *The Third Side*. New York: Penguin Books, 2000.

Weil, Zoe. *Most Good, Least Harm: A Simple Principle for a Better World and Meaningful Life.* New York: Beyond Words/Atria, 2009.

Wrangham, Richard. *The Goodness Paradox: The Strange Relationship Between Virtue and Violence in Human Evolution.* New York: Vintage, 2019.

Yang, Andrew. *The War on Normal People: The Truth About America's Disappearing Jobs and Why Universal Basic Income Is Our Future.* New York: Hachette Books, 2019.

Zaki, Jamil. *The War for Kindness: Building Empathy in a Fractured World.* New York: Crown, 2020.

ORGANIZATIONS AND RESOURCES IN EDUCATION

Algalita: algalita.org/work

Alternative Education Resource Organization: www.educationrevolution.org

Americans Who Tell the Truth: www.americanswhotellthetruth.org

Association for the Advancement of Sustainability in Higher Education: www.aashe.org

Association for Supervision and Curriculum Development (ASCD): www.ascd.org/Default.aspx

Awecademy: www.awecademy.org

BetterLesson: betterlesson.com

Big Picture Learning: www.bigpicture.org

BSCS Science Learning: bscs.org

Buck Institute for Education Project Based Learning: bie.org/about/what_pbl

Ceeds of Peace: ceedsofpeace.org

Center for Compassion and Altruism Research and Education: ccare.stanford.edu

Center for Ecoliteracy: www.ecoliteracy.org

Center for Teaching Quality: www.teachingquality.org

Challenge Success: www.challengesuccess.org

Changemaker Project: www.thechangemakerproject.org

Character Education Partnership (CEP): character.org

Clayton Christensen Institute for Disruptive Innovation: www.christenseninstitute.org

Clear the Air: cleartheaireducation.wordpress.com/about-
     cleartheair
Cloud Institute for Sustainability Education: cloudinstitute.org
Collaborative for Academic, Social and Emotional Learning
     (CASEL): www.casel.org
Creaza: www.creaza.com
Critical Thinking Foundation: www.criticalthinking.org
Critical Thinking Initiative: www.thecriticalthinkinginitiative.org
Curriculum 21 Clearinghouse: www.curriculum21.com/
     clearinghouse
Design for Change: www.dfcworld.com/SITE
Education for Liberation: www.edliberation.org
Education Next: www.educationnext.org
Education to Save the World: edtosavetheworld.com
Education Week: www.edweek.org/ew/index.html
Edutopia: www.edutopia.org
Equity Literacy Institute: www.equityliteracy.org/team
Facing History and Ourselves: www.facinghistory.org
For Each and Every Child: foreachandeverychild.org
Global Future Education Foundation: global-future-
     education.org
Global Oneness Project: www.globalonenessproject.org
Greater Good (education): greatergood.berkeley.edu/
     education
Green Teacher: greenteacher.com
Happy World Foundation: happyworldfoundation.us
HEART: teachhumane.org
Heroic Imagination Project: heroicimagination.org
Human Restoration Project: www.humanrestorationproject.org
Humane Education Coalition: www.hecoalition.org

HundrEd: hundred.org/en

Inspire Citizens: inspirecitizens.org

Institute for Climate and Peace: www.climateandpeace.org

Institute for Democratic Education in America: www.
democraticeducation.org

Institute for Humane Education www.HumaneEducation.org

Khan Academy: www.khanacademy.org

Learning for Justice: www.learningforjustice.org

Map the System: mapthesystem.web.ox.ac.uk/home

Mastery Connect: www.masteryconnect.com

Operation Breaking Stereotypes: www.
operationbreakingstereotypes.org

Partnership for 21st Century Learning: www.p21.org

Peace First: peacefirst.org

Peace Learning Center: peacelearningcenter.org

Progressive Education Network: www.
progressiveeducationnetwork.org

Rethinking Schools: www.rethinkingschools.org/index.shtml

RISE Travel Institute: www.risetravelinstitute.org

River Phoenix Center for Peacebuilding: www.
centerforpeacebuilding.org

Roots and Shoots: www.rootsandshoots.org

SCOPE (Stanford Center for Opportunity Policy in
Education): edpolicy.stanford.edu

Solutionary Athlete: solutionaryathlete.com

Solutionary School: www.thesolutionaryschool.org

Solutions Journalism Network: www.solutionsjournalism.org

Stanford Earth Matters: earth.stanford.edu/earth-matters

Systems-led Leadership: systems-ledleadership.com

Taking IT Global: www.tigweb.org

Teachers Pay Teachers: www.teacherspayteachers.com

Teachers—YouTube: www.youtube.com/user/teachers

Teaching for Change: www.teachingforchange.org

Teach the Future: www.teachthefuture.org

TED-Ed Lessons: ed.ted.com/lessons

Uniting for Kids: www.uniting4kids.com

Uprooting Inequity: uprootinginequity.com

World Citizen: www.peacesites.org

World Peace Game Foundation: www.worldpeacegame.org

World Savvy: www.worldsavvy.org

Worldmapper: worldmapper.org

Yale Center for Emotional Intelligence: ei.yale.edu

Youth Empowered Action: yeacamp.org

YES!: www.yesworld.org

Yes! Magazine for teachers: www.yesmagazine.org/for-teachers

BLOGS AND PODCASTS OF VALUE TO EDUCATORS

Blog21: www.curriculum21.com/blog

Brainwaves Video Anthology: www.youtube.com/user/
     TheBrainwavesChannel

Sam Chaltain: www.samchaltain.com/blog

The Critical Thinking Initiative: www.
     thecriticalthinkinginitiative.org/podcasts

Cult of Pedagogy: www.cultofpedagogy.com

Education Week: www.edweek.org/ew/section/blogs/index.
     html?intc=main-topnav

Ethical Schools Podcast: ethicalschools.org

Jesse Hagopian: iamaneducator.com

Joshua Block: mrjblock.com

Hidden Brain: www.npr.org/series/423302056/hidden-brain

Human Restoration Project: www.humanrestorationproject.
    org/podcast

Institute for Humane Education: humaneeducation.org/blog

Mind Shift: ww2.kqed.org/mindshift

Paul C. Gorski: edchange.org/publications.html

Scott McLeod: dangerouslyirrelevant.org

National Geographic Education Blog: blog.education.
    nationalgeographic.com/about-our-blog

Diane Ravitch: dianeravitch.net

Will Richardson: willrichardson.com/blog

Teach 100 (ranks and conglomerates best education blogs):
    teach.com/teach100

Teach Thought: www.teachthought.com

Teaching to Thrive: podcasts.apple.com/us/podcast/atn-
    teaching-to-thrive/id1525043025

Ten of the best podcasts for teachers: www.weareteachers.
    com/must-listen-podcasts

ACKNOWLEDGMENTS

I am so grateful to the many people who have been involved in various ways with this book and its ideas. There are hundreds of brilliant, insightful teachers and authors whose books and articles I have read (see the Further Reading section), whose presentations I have watched and heard, and who have informed my perspectives about schooling over the many decades I've been an educator. My hope is that this book builds upon and adds to their work.

Many aspects of this book were the result of eighteen months of collaborative work developing ideas and a model for solutionary schools among people connected with the Institute for Humane Education (IHE), including IHE's current and past staff, faculty, board of directors, board of advisors, students, graduates, partners, and colleagues.

Many people read and provided feedback on the first edition as well as this edition. Thank you Victoria Anderson, Liz Behrens, Abba Carmichael, Mary Pat Champeau, Victoria Chiatula, Allan Cohen, Pierce Delahunt, Kathryn Dillon, Mark Doscow, Mary Lee Duff, Susan Feathers, Melissa Feldman, Hope Ferdowsian, Barbara Fiore, Alison Foster, Margery Gallow, Michael Gillis, Bill Gladstone, Chitra Golestani, Lexie Greer, Mark Heimann, Rachel Josephs, Steve Kaufman, Sandra Kleinman, Natalja Lekecinskiene, Dora Lievow, Marion MacGillivray, Dana McPhall, Julie Meltzer, Robyn Moore, Carol Nash, Marsha

Rakestraw, Mark Schulman, Sarah Speare, Kristine Tucker, and Lori Weir. This book was significantly improved because of their combined input. Many thanks, as always, to Martin Rowe at Lantern Publishing & Media. Martin suggested crowd-sourcing feedback to the first draft of this book, a wonderful way to learn from many people, and make changes based on multiple perspectives.

Finally, and always, my deepest gratitude to my husband, Edwin Barkdoll, and son, Forest Barkdoll-Weil, both of whom also read and critiqued this book. Forest did so on Mother's Day, which was the perfect mother's day gift.

ABOUT THE INSTITUTE FOR HUMANE EDUCATION

www.HumaneEducation.org

The Institute for Humane Education (IHE) offers free resources, professional development opportunities, and online graduate programs with Antioch University for teachers and change-makers who want to create a more just, humane, and sustainable future by educating about the interconnected issues of human rights, environmental sustainability, and animal protection and building a society of solutionaries.

Our Mission

IHE educates people to create a world in which all humans, animals, and nature can thrive.

Our Strategy

- **Online M.Ed., M.A., Ed.D., and Graduate Certificate programs**, delivered in partnership with Antioch University and designed to prepare teachers and change-makers to educate about the interconnected issues of human rights, environmental sustainability, and animal protection and help others to become solutionaries.
- **A Solutionary Hub** that provides opportunities for learning, a Solutionary Micro-credential Program for teachers, free resources, and methodologies for advancing the growing solutionary movement.

- **High Impact Outreach** through keynote addresses, books, articles, workshops, TEDx talks, and consultation.

ABOUT THE AUTHOR

Photograph by Forest Barkdoll-Weil

Zoe Weil is the co-founder and president of the **Institute for Humane Education (IHE)** and is considered a pioneer in the comprehensive humane education movement that works to create a peaceful, regenerative, and equitable world. Zoe created IHE's online **graduate** programs as well as IHE's acclaimed **workshops** and online professional development opportunities.

Zoe is the author of Nautilus Silver Medal winner, *Most Good, Least Harm: A Simple Principle for a Better World and Meaningful Life* (2009), *The Power and Promise of Humane Education* (2004), and *Above All, Be Kind: Raising a Humane Child in Challenging Times* (2003). She has also written books for young people, including Moonbeam Gold Medal winner, *Claude and Medea* (2007), about twelve-year-old activists inspired by their teacher to right wrongs where they find them, and *So, You Love Animals: An Action-Packed, Fun-Filled Book to Help Kids Help Animals* (1994). She has written numerous articles and book chapters on humane education and humane and sustainable living and writes the blog "Becoming a Solutionary" at *Psychology Today*.

In 2010, Zoe gave her first TEDx talk "The World Becomes What You Teach," which became among the fifty top-rated TEDx talks within a year of upload. Since then, she has given other TEDx talks, including "Solutionaries," "Educating for Freedom," "How to be a Solutionary," "Extending Our Circle of Compassion," and "How Will You Answer This Question?"

Zoe speaks regularly at universities, conferences, and schools across the United States and Canada as well as overseas. She has served as a consultant on humane education to people and organizations around the world, and her vision has become the model for the first solutionary school in India.

In 2012, Zoe debuted her one-woman show, "My Ongoing Problems with Kindness: Confessions of MOGO Girl," bringing humane issues to communities through comedy. That same year, she was honored with the Women in Environmental Leadership award from Unity College, and her portrait was painted by Robert Shetterly for the *Americans Who Tell The Truth* portrait series. In 2020 she and IHE were featured in the Apple TV+ episode 7 "Dear . . ." series and in the film *8 Billion Angels*.

Zoe received a Master's in Theological Studies from Harvard Divinity School (1988) and a Master's and Bachelor's in English Literature from the University of

Pennsylvania (1983). In 2015, she was awarded an honorary Doctor of Humanities degree from Valparaiso University. Zoe is certified in Psychosynthesis counseling, a form of psychotherapy which relies upon the intrinsic power of each person's imagination to promote growth, creativity, health, and transformation. She's also a graduate of the Maine Master Naturalist Program.

Zoe lives with her husband and rescued animals on the coast of Maine, where she can often be found exploring and taking photographs in nature.

ABOUT THE PUBLISHER

LANTERN PUBLISHING & MEDIA was founded in 2020 to follow and expand on the legacy of Lantern Books—a publishing company started in 1999 on the principles of living with a greater depth and commitment to the preservation of the natural world. Like its predecessor, Lantern Publishing & Media produces books on animal advocacy, veganism, religion, social justice, and psychology and family therapy. Lantern is dedicated to printing in the United States on recycled paper and saving resources in our day-to-day operations. Our titles are also available as e-books and audiobooks.

To catch up on Lantern's publishing program, visit us at www.lanternpm.org.

facebook.com/lanternpm
twitter.com/lanternpm
instagram.com/lanternpm